THE PAPERS OF ADAM HAMLETT

By: Adam Hamlett

Introduction

Discover the inaugural edition of the remarkable writings of Adam Hamlett, a distinguished academic hailing from the historic town of Appomattox, Virginia. Aspiring to achieve his juris doctorate, Hamlett offers readers a unique glimpse into his intellectual journey.

This captivating collection features a selection of meticulously crafted academic works and legal assignments, thoughtfully edited to maintain client confidentiality. While this edition serves as an intriguing introduction to Hamlett's scholarly endeavors, it is merely a prelude to the comprehensive compilation set to be unveiled at the end of next year.

Please note that this book is incomplete and the writings herein are mostly random – upon graduation I will organize this document better so that it may be enjoyed to the fullest.

Immerse yourself in the compelling narratives and insightful analyses that define Adam Hamlett's burgeoning legal mind, and join him on his path to academic and professional excellence.

MEMORANDUM

I.   Introduction

This memo analyzes Liberty University's potential liability for possession of an outside company's trade secrets. This memo addresses the obligations the University has to return such property and whether it can, in turn demand return of property it considers to be confidential. The memo also addresses potential civil and criminal claims within the context of failing to comply with the received demand. It also contemplates whether the University can comply with a request to destroy data in its possession pursuant to the demand without violating any evidence spoliation laws.

II.   Questions Presented

1.   Assuming this is a possession of stolen property matter, what are the obligations under Virginia law for both parties when they are on notice that they are in possession of property; can the possessor of stolen property insist on a reciprocal return?

2.   Should Liberty refuse to comply with the demand, what civil claims are available to a plaintiff in this matter?

3.   Should Liberty refuse to comply with the demand, what are the available criminal consequences for such inaction?

4.   How does evidence and spoliation law consider the destruction of confidential data once copies have been returned to a third party at that party's demand?

III.   Short Answers

1.   There is no explicit requirement that Liberty return the data under existing state law and thus conditioning return on reciprocal exchange is not prohibited by such laws.

2.   The authority on the matter suggests a plaintiff would have remedies available under Virginia's Uniform Trade Secrets Act, the Defending Trade Secrets Act, and common law conversion.

3.   There are few criminal sanctions that could apply to Liberty at large, however certain criminal sanctions may be appliable against individuals that are employed by the university.

4.   Should Liberty choose to destroy copies of the data after complying with a demand for its return, it is unlikely that it would face sanctions under either of the two accepted standards for spoliation of evidence.

IV.   Statement of Facts:

The allegations are that during the recruiting and hiring process of an employee for an in-house investment position at Liberty, the potential then future employee had communications with his supervisor to be. He furnished her several documents concerning the investment assets and portfolio performance of his last employer and she furnished him some confidential documents of Liberty University regarding its investment assets and portfolio performance. The former employer says it did an investigation of the former employee's email and discovered this transfer of data after he left. It considered the information shared without its consent to be confidential, trade secret and proprietary, and its property.

The attorney sent a letter outlining the facts, providing the dates and times of the emails and demanded the immediate identification and return of all of its documents and materials in the possession of Liberty and destruction of all copies not able to be returned. The attorney also demanded that Liberty image the employees' computers and put holds on their emails and electronic data (including documents) to prevent their destruction or deletion and any spoliation of evidence; Liberty has complied with this request.

V.   Discussion

a. The return of stolen property under state law.

Virginia law does not explicitly require a party to return confidential trade secrets they are in possession of to the rightful owner. However, the Virginia Uniform Trade Secrets Act (VUTSA) does prohibit the improper acquisition of a trade secret, regardless of whether the secret is used in direct competition with the rightful owner Va. Code Ann. § 59.1-336. Under the Act, the return of such data is therefore not mandatory.

However, assuming this is a possession of stolen property matter, the analysis may turn into a question surrounding he unconditional intent doctrine found in state larceny statutes. In the context of Virginia law, the return of stolen physical property does not necessarily absolve an individual of larceny charges. The intent at the time of the taking is a crucial factor. If the individual intended to permanently deprive the owner of the property at the time of the theft, the act can be considered larceny, even if the property was later returned. Va. Code Ann. § 6-116.

The intent to return the property must be unconditional. If the taker intends to return the property only if he should receive a reward for its return, or only upon some other condition which he has no right to impose, it is no defense to larceny. The intent with

4

Comment [DC]: Here we are dealing with stealing a copy. So can I conclude that no one was intending toe deprive owner of the property as the owner still had all the copies it had created. The only way I could see an argument is if you say the ownership interest in a trade secret is EXCLUSIVE possession and by taking a copy and intending to keep it, one has intended to permanently deprive the owner of exclusive possession of the trade secret—its no longer "secret". Thoughs?

which the property is taken at the time of its taking determines the offense. In determining intent, the factfinder may consider the conduct of the person involved and all circumstances revealed by evidence. Va. Code Ann. § 6-116.

However, in reviewing the applicable case law, there is no prevailing authority within the state of Virginia that has considered the idea of reciprocal return of stolen data or property, especially where the trade secret is in the form of a copy of a document that does not deprive the owner of the original and copies remaining in the owner's possession. Here, assuming that the data here truly is a trade secret, the act governing the possession of such data does not mandate its return to it owner. Given the lack of clarity in the law Liberty is not necessarily required to return the trade secrets it now possesses but a return would tend to limit damages that could be claimed from ongoing possession. Further, absent any other conditions, insisting on a reciprocal return of data in this matter is not prohibited by law and since in occurs after the fact, is not relevant to whether there was an intent to permanently deprive or to return at the time of taking.

b. The available civil remedies under federal and state law.

With the facts presented, the potential plaintiff in this matter could assert two claims for trade secret misappropriation and one state law claim for conversion. The state claim falls under the Uniform Trade Secret Act of Virginia found in Va. Conde Ann. §§ 59.1-336 — 59.1-343. The appropriate claim under that title would be misappropriation of a trade secret. The federal claim, also for misappropriation is found in 18 U.S.C. § 1836. And lastly, the conversion claim will be analyzed under state common law from Virginia; each of these claims will be discussed in turn below.

The Uniform Trade Secrets Act of Virginia only penalizes actors who misappropriate the trade secrets of another. The act states,

> "Misappropriation means . . . acquisition of a trade secret of another by a person who knows or has reason to know that the trade secret was acquired by improper means or use of a trade secret of another without express or implied consent by a person who . . . at the time of disclosure or use, knew or had reason to know that his knowledge of the trade secret was derived from or through a person who had utilized improper means to acquire it; or acquired by accident or mistake." Va. Code Ann. § 59.1-336

Under the Virginia law, a plaintiff is entitled to recover damages for its loss. Damages can include both the actual loss caused by misappropriation and the unjust enrichment caused by misappropriation that is not taken into account in computing actual loss. Va Code Ann. § 59.1-338 (a). If the plaintiff is unable to assess damages in the tradition sense, the court may award damages in the form a reasonable royalty upon the benefits of the trade secret's misappropriation. Id. If willful and malicious misappropriation exists, the court may award punitive damages in an amount not exceeding twice any award of compensatory damages or $350,000, whichever amount is less. Va Code Ann. § 59.1-338 (b).

Under Virginia law, the mere acquisition of trade secrets, if unintentional or inadvertent, does not necessarily constitute misappropriation. Pais v. Automation Prods., 36 Va. Cir. 230; Babcock & Wilcox Co. v. Areva NP, Inc, 292 Va. 165. In the context of a company interviewing a person and learning information deemed to be a trade secret, the company would not be liable for misappropriation unless it used or disclosed the trade secret without consent and knew or had reason to know that the trade secret was acquired under circumstances giving rise to a duty to maintain its secrecy or limit its use. For instance, if the company knew that the person being interviewed had a duty to maintain the secrecy of the trade secret and still proceeded to use or disclose the information, the company could potentially be held liable for misappropriation. *See* Trade Secret Protection (VA)MicroStrategy Inc. v. Li, 268 Va. 249. However, if the company merely learned the trade secret during the interview and did not use or disclose the information, it would not be liable for misappropriation under the Virginia Uniform Trade Secrets Act. This is because the Act does not affect a person who properly acquires trade secrets and merely holds them without any actual or threatened disclosure or use.

Here, a plaintiff's argument establishing a claim under state law would turn on Liberty's knowledge of the data it received, the purpose for which it was acquired, and whether Liberty has used the trade secret to its advantage or disclosed the trade secret. If Liberty knew or reasonably should have known the information it received was a trade secret it could be exposed to liability. Further investigation of the acquiring employee's understanding, intent, handling and use of the data given by the employee is essential to assessing Liberty's potential liability. However, Liberty is now on notice that the actions of this employee are alleged to be improper and thus if Liberty is currently using the data to its advantage, it may be liable under the Act because now the University has the requisite knowledge for plaintiff to state a claim under state law.

The University may also be liable under the federal Defending Trade Secrets Act found in 18 U.S.C. § 1836. Such an action will only lie if, "the trade secret is related to a product or service used in, or intended for use in, interstate or foreign commerce." 18 U.S.C. § 1836 (b)(1). Under federal law, misappropriation is defined in the same manner as Virginia state law. 18 U.S.C. § 1839 (5). And thus, similarly to the state claim above, the mere acquisition of trade secrets, if unintentional or inadvertent, does not necessarily

Comment [DC]: Is this part of the citation?

constitute misappropriation under federal law. A federal court can also award damages for actual loss caused by the misappropriation of the trade secret and may award damages in the form a reasonable royalty; punitive damages are appropriate if the trade secret is willfully and maliciously misappropriated; and the award must not more than double the value of compensatory damages. 18 U.S.C. § 1836 (b)(3).

Under the federal Act, the argument would be the same as the state law claim above. Again, there would have to be an exploration of whether there is any factual basis to establish that Liberty initially knew the data given by the employee was acquired by improper means or even that it was confidential. And since Liberty is now on notice that the actions of this employee are alleged to be improper, if Liberty is currently using the data to its advantage, it may well be liable under the federal Act because now the University has the requisite knowledge for plaintiff to also state a valid federal claim.

Lastly, the plaintiff would have a cause of action for conversion under the common law of Virginia. To assert a claim for conversion, a plaintiff must prove by a preponderance of the evidence (1) the ownership or right to possession of the property at the time of the conversion and (2) the wrongful exercise of dominion or control by the defendant over the plaintiff's property, thus depriving the plaintiff of possession. Airlines Reporting Corp. v. Pishvaian, 155 F. Supp. 2d 659 (E.D.Va.1997). Moreover, an action for conversion can be maintained only by one who has a property interest in and is entitled to the immediate possession of the thing alleged to be wrongfully converted. United Leasing Corp., 247 Va. at 305 (citing Mullins v. Sutherland, 131 Va. 547 (1921)). When the conversion is complete, the measure of damages, generally, is the value of the property converted at the time and the place of conversion. Straley v. Fisher, 176 Va. 163 (1940).

A cause of action for conversion typically applies only to tangible property. However, the conversion of intangible property rights that arise from or are merged with a document, such as a valid stock certificate, promissory note, or bond have been recognized. To establish a conversion of intangibles, however, the plaintiff must have both a property interest in and be entitled to immediate possession of the documented intangible property. For that reason, the supreme court has refused to recognize a conversion claim for interference with undocumented intangible property rights. Only a clear, definite, undisputed, and obvious property right in a thing to which the plaintiffs are entitled to immediate possession is sufficient to support a claim for conversion. Mackey v. McDannald, 298 Va. 645 (2020).

Here, the potential plaintiff may have a valid cause of action for the data it seeks returned. At some point, the data Liberty possesses was likely physically printed financial data. Thus, the electronic intellectual property here was at some point tangible and converted to a print medium. Furthermore, the plaintiff in this matter would clearly have a possessory right over its own confidential information. Liberty also has no right to possess the data, especially now that it is on notice of its true ownership and that the owner never consented to its disclosure to the school. It would therefore appear that plaintiff is fully entitled to the return of its property and therefore the necessary elements of conversion in Virginia appear to have been met.

However, there is also the possibility that Liberty could raise a preemption argument against any conversion claim. The Uniform Trade Secrets Act of Virginia provides, "this chapter displaces conflicting tort, restitutionary, and other law of this Commonwealth providing civil remedies for misappropriation of a trade secret." Va. Code Ann. § 59.1-341 (a). Several defendants have attempted to argue that conversion claims are preempted by the statute. While courts appear split on the issue, the general principle is that for a conversion claim to be preempted under the statute the claim must be premised entirely upon the alleged misappropriation of trade secrets. TK Elevator Corp. v. Shropshire, No. 7:21-CV-00579, 2022 WL 564648 (W.D. Va. Feb. 23, 2022).

Here, given that the property sought is primarily in dispute because of its confidential trade secret status, this preemption argument is valid. However, if plaintiff could plead and establish that the conversion claim that stands on its own absent any confidential or proprietary element, the preemption argument would fail.

c. **The potential criminal sanctions:**

Generally speaking, the law in regard to prosecuting companies for theft is complex in Virginia. The main question would be defining what a "person" is under applicable state law. There are a few cases in which a corporation has been considered to be a "person" under the law, but this was in the context of being a victim of a crime, not the commission of a crime. See Waters v. Commonwealth, 29 Va. App. 133 (1999). However, assuming arguendo that both Liberty and its employees can be prosecuted, the two most likely crimes applicable here are receiving stolen property and grand larceny.

Grand larceny can be charged when property is either taken from another's person or their possession. Va. Code Ann. § 18.2-95. Given that the victim here would be a corporate entity, the larceny could not be from its "person." The law states specifically, "Any person who . . . commits simple larceny not from the person of another of goods and chattels of the value of $1,000 or more . . . shall be guilty of grand larceny." Id. For clarity, simple larceny is defined as, "the wrongful or fraudulent taking of personal goods of some intrinsic value, belonging to another, without his assent, and with the intention to deprive the owner thereof permanently." Foster v. Commonwealth, 44 Va. App. 574(2004). Likewise, a victim under this statue can be a corporate entity. See Waters, 29 Va. App. 133.

Here, it is likely that the employee in this matter could be prosecuted for this crime. However, this is an assumption that the value of the trade secret is at or over $1,000 and that the requisite elements of simple larceny are met. Of course, the intent of the employees would be important here; the focus could be whether the sending employee even knew the files he sent were not his to take, a fairly safe assumption. Less clear is whether the receiving employee knew the files she received were not the sender's to send, which also seems likely but would be fact dependent. Whether knowledge of the employees in question could be imputed to the university is outside the scope of this memorandum. If convicted of grand larceny under the statute the employee or university could face, "imprisonment in a state correctional facility for not less than one nor more than 20 years or, in the discretion of the jury or court trying the case without a jury, be confined in jail for a period not exceeding 12 months or fined not more than $2,500, either or both." Va. Code Ann. § 18.2-95.

A similar crime that may apply to the University or to other employees is the crime of receiving stolen property. Virginia law states, "If any person . . . receives from another person, or aids in concealing, any stolen goods or other thing, knowing the same to have been stolen, he shall be deemed guilty of larceny thereof." Va. Code Ann. § 18.2-108. This crime will be considered punishable as grand larceny if the value of the goods is over $1,000. Va. Code Ann. § 18.2-95.

Here, as above, the issue of knowledge would be key. The question is whether Liberty or its employees knew that the data given during and after the interview process was stolen property. Moreover, given that the University is now on notice that the "goods" are considered to be stolen, any attempt to conceal or prevent recovery by the afflicted party may result in prosecution.

d. The Spoliation Dilemma

Spoliation is "the destruction or material alteration of evidence or to the failure to preserve property for another's use as evidence in pending or reasonably foreseeable litigation." Silvestri v. Gen. Motors Corp., 271 F.3d 583, 590 (4th Cir. 2001). A court's power to sanction spoliation derives from two sources: (1) Fed. R. Civ. P. 37(e); and (2) its "inherent power . . . to redress conduct 'which abuses the judicial process.'" Id. However, "the applicable sanction should be molded to serve the prophylactic, punitive, and remedial rationales underlying the spoliation doctrine." Silvestri, 271 F.3d at 590. Appropriate purposes include: "'(1) deter[ring] parties from engaging in spoliation; (2) plac[ing] the risk of an erroneous judgment on the party who wrongfully created the risk; and (3) restor[ing] the prejudiced party to the same position he would have been in absent the wrongful destruction of evidence by the opposing party.'" West v. Goodyear Tire & Rubber Co., 167 F.3d 776, 779 (2d Cir. 1999). The rule states,

> "If electronically stored information that should have been preserved in the anticipation or conduct of litigation is lost because a party failed to take reasonable steps to preserve it, and it cannot be restored or replaced through additional discovery, the court:
> (1) upon finding prejudice to another party from loss of the information, may order measures no greater than necessary to cure the prejudice; or
> (2) only upon finding that the party acted with the intent to deprive another party of the information's use in the litigation may:
> > (A) presume that the lost information was unfavorable to the party;
> > (B) instruct the jury that it may or must presume the information was unfavorable to the party; or
> > (C) dismiss the action or enter a default judgment."

Fed. R. Civ. P. 37.

Thus, a movant must satisfy four threshold requirements before a court decides if any spoliation sanction is appropriate: (1) ESI should have been preserved; (2) ESI was lost; (3) the loss was due to a party's failure to take reasonable steps to preserve the ESI; and (4) the ESI cannot be restored or replaced through additional discovery. Steves & Sons, Inc. v. Jeld-Wen, Inc., 327 F.R.D. 96 (E.D. Va. 2018).

Moving to the inherent power of a court to enter sanctions regardless of the inapplicable nature of Rule 37, the party seeking sanctions must show: "'(1) [t]he party having control over the evidence had an obligation to preserve it when it was destroyed or altered; (2) [t]he destruction or loss was accompanied by a culpable state of mind; and (3) [t]he evidence that was destroyed or altered was relevant to the claims or defenses of the party that sought the discovery. Steves & Sons, Inc. v. Jeld-Wen, Inc., 327 F.R.D. 96 (E.D. Va. 2018). Under the facts, it seems no sanctions would be available against Liberty under either the Federal Rules or the court's inherent powers under the common law.

In Jeld-Wen, the Defendant ordered deletion of data that it considered to confidential property of the plaintiff and potentially problematic for his company. Id. at 102. As such, meeting notes, emails, and other internal documents were deleted by defendant before a discovery order was received and before a lawsuit was filed. Id. Once the suit was filed, plaintiff sought sanctions for spoliation under Rule 37 and under common law. Id.

The court denied the motion for sanctions. Id. at 111. The court reasoned that under the common law and Rule 37, the plaintiff had not met his burden to show the ESI was irrecoverable or irreplaceable because the plaintiff had the same communications in its own records. Id. at 109. For that reason, among other failings in the filing (a failure to show harm) the court denied the motion for sanctions.

Here, any claim by a potential plaintiff that the University spoliated evidence of its trade secrets being in its passion and the possession of its employees by destroying copies at the request of the potential plaintiff would be unfounded. Turning to the threshold requirements the latter two may not be met in this scenario. Any loss here would not be due to a failure to take reasonable precaution on the University's part; the potential plaintiff in this matter demanded that the data be deleted upon prompt return. Similarly like the communications in Jeld-Wen, the fourth requirement may not be met because plaintiff has access to emails sent to Liberty that allegedly contain the improper information, it has evidence of Liberty's possession of the data in question. For those two reasons alone, Rule 37 and the court's inherent sanctions power cannot provide an avenue for sanctions against the University.

VI.   Conclusion

Regarding the university's concerns about return of potential trade secrets following a demand received by the University: First, an analysis of the relevant law and practical considerations indicates requiring a reciprocal return of data held by both parties is permissible. Second, failure to comply with the demand could result in federal and state claims for misappropriation, as well as additional claims for conversion. Potential criminal sanctions for larceny and receipt of stolen property may be applicable depending on how the facts develop. Finally, it was determined that the destruction of the data pursuant to a demand by its owner following return of copies is permissible under spoliation law without sanction.

Memorandum Concerning Vaccines – July 2024

I.   Introduction

This memorandum addresses whether the client can completely end the recognition of religious exemptions from its vaccine policies in its medical programs (nursing, medicine, etc). Students at private universities have significantly less legal protection that students at public universities. Federal law under Title II, IV, and VII do not apply for various reasons. Ronald J. Colombo, *When Exemptions Discriminate: Unlawfully Narrow Religious Exemptions to Vaccination Mandates by Private Colleges and Universities*, 44 W. New Eng. L. Rev. 293 (2022). Likewise, federal Constitutional protections are likely inapplicable in these circumstances. *Id.* Further, Virginia state law mandating exemptions for religious reasons only apply to public degree granting institutions. Va. Code Ann § 23.1-800. For these reasons, this memorandum concludes that the client could purse its desired cause of action with little legal risk.

However, such a course of action would put Liberty University on a rather lonely island. A survey of various religious private universities reveals that none have taken the action the client suggests; in fact, many such schools join in the other extreme, granting vast exemptions in mass or simply not requiring vaccination at all. In turn, the client should consider this when determining what course of action it will take in this matter.

II.   Questions Presented

1.   What inherent legal risks would emerge if the client chose to deny religious exemptions to vaccination in their entirety within its medical programs?

2.   What are the general practices of other private religious institutions concerning vaccination exemption policies?

III.   Short Answers:

1.   Because of the private nature of Liberty University, the vast majority of federal and state prohibitions do not apply in this scenario and any that do apply are unlikely to succeed.

2.   Liberty University would stand entirely alone if the questioned action here is taken, the majority of religious private universities either provide exemptions or do not require vaccination at all.

IV.   Discussion:
a. The Legal Risks of the Suggested Conduct:

Students at private religious schools surrender many federal protections that they would otherwise possess at a public university. There are two simple reasons for this. The first is that, as private institutions, such colleges and universities are not organs or instrumentalities of the government. This removes them from the reach of the protections enshrined in the U.S. Constitution. Under the "state action doctrine," private institutions can, under certain circumstances, be treated like government actors for constitutional purposes. *Heineke v. Santa Clara Univ.*, 965 F.3d 1009 (9th Cir. 2020). This doctrine, however, has been ill-defined and unpredictably applied, prompting one commentator to write: "There is little coherence to the Supreme Court's State action jurisprudence." *See* Eric Sirota, *Can the First Amendment Save Net Neutrality?* 70 BAYLOR L. REV. 781, 841 (2018). In any event, it is extremely unlikely that the doctrine could ever be applied to a private school in in one of these cases as the mere receipt of federal funds does not create a state actor. *Heineke*, 965 F.3d at 1012.

Second, the majority of federal civil rights law was not legislated with private universities in mind. For example, Title VI provides, "No person in the United States shall, on the ground of race, color, or national origin, be excluded from participation in, be denied the benefits of, or be subjected to discrimination under any program or activity receiving Federal financial assistance." 42 U.S.C. § 2000d. However, noticeably absent from these protections is any mention of religion as a protected class. This appears to be an intentional action on the part of congress as there was some concern over how the regulation would affect religious schools. *See* Kenneth L. Marcus, *The Most Important Right We Think We Have but Don't: Freedom from Religious Discrimination in Education*, 7 NEV. L.J. 171, 174 (2006).

In contrast to the treatment of students, employees are protected from religious discrimination under Title VII of the Civil Rights Act, and thus would be entitled to a religious exception. 42. U.S.C. § 2000e-2. Likewise, all persons are protected from religious discrimination in places of public accommodation under Title II of the Civil Rights Act.

Although "public accommodation" may be a better avenue for a litigious student, that term has been narrowly interpreted to cover only "five categories of establishments: 'lodgings; facilities principally engaged in selling food for consumption on the premises; gasoline stations; places of exhibition or entertainment;' and establishments located within covered establishments and open to the public." 42 U.S.C. § 2000a. Students who suffer from religious discrimination with regard to university housing, dormitories, and eateries would appear to have a cause of action against a wrongdoer under Title II, but this question has not been resolved definitively. *See* Elizabeth Sepper, *The Role of Religion in State Public Accommodations Laws*, 60 ST. LOUIS U. L.J. 631, 639–40 (2016). Virginia has a similar statute, but neither the federal nor the state law seem applicable to this scenario. Va. Code Ann. § 2.2-3900(1).

Turning to Virginia state law, it is clear there is no statutory requirement to provide exemptions for religious reasons in the context of a private institution. State law provides, "Prior to enrollment for the first time in any baccalaureate *public institution* of higher education, each student shall be immunized by vaccine against diphtheria, tetanus, poliomyelitis, measles (rubeola), German measles (rubella), and mumps according to the guidelines of the American College Health Association." Va. Code. Ann. § 23.1-800(b). This statute does mandate a religious exemption but does not apply to private institutions. *Id*.

Based on the legal analysis, it is clear that there are no significant legal barriers preventing the client from eliminating religious exemptions for vaccines in its medical programs. The key federal protections against religious discrimination do not apply to private institutions in this context, and there is no evidence of intent to discriminate by uniformly denying religious exemptions. Both federal and state laws allow private entities considerable autonomy in setting their own policies, including vaccination requirements. Therefore, the client's proposed policy to end religious exemptions for vaccines within its medical programs does not present substantial legal risks.

b. **A survey of vaccination polices of various private institutions:**

To better understand the landscape of vaccination exemption policies among private religious institutions, this section surveys a variety of schools to identify common practices and noteworthy differences. Many private religious universities offer exemptions for vaccinations on religious grounds, reflecting their commitment to accommodating the diverse beliefs of their student populations. However, some institutions, prioritizing public health, restrict exemptions primarily to medical reasons. By examining the policies of these schools, we can provide a comprehensive overview that will inform Liberty University's decision-making process regarding vaccination requirements. This survey includes examples from Brigham Young University, Regent University, Notre Dame University, Pepperdine University, Baylor University, Southern Methodist University, and Duke University, each illustrating different approaches to balancing religious accommodation and public health.

On one end of the spectrum, Brigham Young University (BYU) and Regent University do not mandate vaccinations for COVID-19 or other standard diseases for their students. These schools, however, emphasize the importance of vaccinations by linking to CDC compliance sites and strongly encouraging students to get vaccinated for standard diseases. This approach allows students to make their own decisions while providing them with information on the benefits of vaccination.

Conversely, it is more common for private institutions to require vaccinations but allow for religious exemptions. For instance, Notre Dame University mandates vaccinations but provides an exemption process that requires students to submit a detailed explanation for their exemption requests. The necessary form is available online and must be completed thoroughly to be considered. Pepperdine University has a similar policy. Their COVID-19 vaccination policy requires all students to be vaccinated unless they claim an exemption. The exemption process involves filling out a form via the Student Health Center Patient Portal for medical, religious, or philosophical reasons. Although this form is not publicly accessible, the university ensures that students can apply for exemptions as needed.

Baylor University and Southern Methodist University (SMU) also mandate vaccinations while allowing religious exemptions. Both universities require students to submit documentation supporting their exemption requests, thereby accommodating religious beliefs while maintaining overall public health standards on campus. On the other hand, some universities, such as Stanford and Duke, primarily provide information on medical exemptions online. Their websites include exemption forms for various vaccines, but these forms are generally inaccessible to the public. These institutions emphasize medical exemptions while offering limited publicly available information on religious or philosophical exemptions.

The survey of vaccination exemption policies among private religious institutions highlights a range of approaches, from not mandating vaccinations to requiring them but allowing religious exemptions. If Liberty University were to choose to uniformly deny religious exemptions for vaccinations, it would be an outlier among private religious institutions. The common practice is to allow for religious exemptions, ensuring that the diverse beliefs of the student population are accommodated while striving to protect public health. Denying religious exemptions could place Liberty University on a "lonely island," as it would be one of the few private religious institutions taking such a stance. This comprehensive overview should inform Liberty University's decision-making process, highlighting the legal and ethical considerations of vaccination exemption policies and the prevailing practices among peer institutions.

V.   Conclusion

This memorandum addressed the potential for Liberty University to eliminate religious exemptions from its vaccine policies within its medical programs. The legal analysis indicates that private universities like Liberty University are not subject to the same federal and state prohibitions that apply to public institutions. Federal laws under Title II, IV, and VII, as well as Virginia state laws, do not mandate religious exemptions for private universities. Therefore, Liberty University faces minimal legal risk in pursuing this policy change.

However, if Liberty University were to eliminate religious exemptions entirely, it would stand alone among private religious institutions. The prevalent practice is to accommodate religious beliefs while ensuring the health and safety of the campus community. Denying religious exemptions could place Liberty University on a "lonely island," highlighting a significant deviation from the norms observed at peer institutions.

<u>Worldviews and Human Cloning Fall 2023</u>

Introduction:

In 1996 Ian Wilmut successfully cloned a sheep from an adult somatic cell. The scientific community and the world at large were immediately forced to consider new and complex moral qualms about the possibilities of cloning. In the last two decades, the practice has grown in many ways. After sheep, companies began to clone other animals; these companies now can clone small pets with around a thirty percent success rate.[1] While no human has successfully been born as a result of reproductive cloning, the process is scientifically feasible.[2] The Chair of the Global

---

[1]Viagen Pets, (Oct. 9, 2023, 9:34 AM), https://www.viagenpets.com/
[2] Ayala, Francisco J. *Cloning humans? Biological, Ethical, and Social Considerations*, 112 Proc. of the Nat'l Acad. of Sci. of the U.S. 29 (2015)

23

Board of The Nature Conservancy, Bill Frist, summarizes the essence of the modern debate surrounding the practice, "This cloning debate . . . forces us to address what is inevitable as we look to the future, and that is a rapid-fire, one-after-another onslaught of new scientific-technological innovation that has to be assimilated into our ethical-social fabric . . . science and ethics must march hand in hand."[3]

Both secular and religious communities have long held distinct worldviews that inform their mindset as to many issues prevalent in modern society. However, in perhaps an odd occurrence, cloning is one area where both secular and religious communities generally agree that the practice is immoral. As such, the views of the most prominent religious movements worldwide will be discussed. The goal will be to reconcile the schools of thought and explain the profound moral objections that religious communities worldwide have to the practice of cloning.

The secular and Western scientific community has also raised valid concerns about the process. They remained concerned about the potential for harm to be caused to cloned individuals, autonomy issues, and mental health concerns. However, notably, there is a growing minority in the secular scientific community that will be addressed in turn. The secular and religious governments worldwide have also adopted positive laws to address the issue; however, in many countries, like the United States, no such law exists on the subject. Given the moral qualms presented by both secular and religious groups, this paper will establish a survey of the prevailing views on both the religious and secular views on the topic of human cloning, the present law surrounding the issue, and further propose a solution to the ethical and moral qualms it presents.

---

[3] Bill Frist, *Twenty-Five Years After My House Call To Dolly: What Have We Learned About Cloning And How Did We Learn It,* Forbes, (Oct. 9, 2023, 9:34 AM) https://www.forbes.com/sites/billfrist/2022/08/02/twenty-five-years-after-my-house-call-to-dolly-what-have-we-learned-about-cloning-and-how-did-we-learn-it/?sh=66cfb18759c0 (2022)

The Scope of this Writing:

Cloning as a whole is a complex science that has many different claimed purposes. Two main types of human cloning are potentially relevant here; therapeutic cloning and reproductive cloning. In therapeutic cloning, an embryo is created and the resulting "cloned" cells remain in a dish in a lab; they are not implanted into a female's uterus. Conversely, reproductive cloning, the focus of this article, involves the cloned embryo being placed in the uterine environment where it will continue to grow until birth. While there is a general agreement among secular groups that reproductive cloning at this time is unethical, there is some level of disagreement as to the ethics around therapeutic cloning. For this writing, any activity referred to as cloning should be understood to mean reproductive cloning.

Secular Concerns:

The arguments against cloning that populate secular thought revolve around ethical concerns with, the risk of harm, mental health, and the parent-child relationship; mostly aspects that would affect the cloned individual. While the debate is both vigorous and diverse, the general conclusion is that the practice of cloning is not ethical at this time. However, there is a growing minority that stands for the position that the practice ought to be allowed; both will be discussed here.

a) **Risk of Physical Harm:**
Bodily autonomy has dominated the field of modern bioethics. First introduced to the field following the Nuremberg Trials, many secular scholars consider the concept of doing no harm to be essential in experimentation and treatment. The aforementioned Nuremberg Code provides, "The experiment should be so conducted as to avoid all unnecessary physical and

mental suffering and injury."[4] This principle has been adopted as "cause no harm." However, there is considerable disagreement as to what the definition of harm is.

One standard view defines harm as the worsening of one's situation and requires an essential balancing of the benefits of a given action.[5] Shiffrin, a professor of law and philosophy at the University of California explains, "What we classify as harms must be the sorts of things that could reliably give rise to a reason to avoid, prevent, or alleviate them consistent with our maintaining the social and interpersonal conditions of meaningful autonomy."[6] This view appears to prevail in most circles; the risks of physical harm in cloning will be analyzed using this standard.

There is some significant debate as to the amount of harm that can be caused to the cloned individual after such conception. Firstly, reproductive cloning currently has a relatively low success rate that sits at around five percent for familiar species and around one percent for unfamiliar species.[7] The concern, perhaps an appropriate one, is whether there will be a higher success rate once such methods are used on humans. The secular school of thought would most certainly take issue with the death or deformed appearance of ninety-five out of every hundred potential lives born by reproductive cloning. Even taking the complex arguments against when life begins, there would still be significant death as a result of any mass cloning attempt at present. As such, the resulting death would certainly be considered a "great harm" as defined in the modern field of bioethics. Such harm is understood to be unethical.

---

[4] *United States v. Karl Brandt, et all* (Nov. 21, 1946 – Aug. 20, 1947)

[5] Shiffrin, S, *Harm and its Moral Significance*. 18 Legal Theory 357-398 (2012).

[6] *Id.*

[7] Ferris Jabr, *Will Cloning Ever Save Endangered Animals?*, Scientific American, (Oct. 9, 2023, 2:50 PM), https://www.scientificamerican.com/article/cloning-endangeredanimals/#:~:text=Now%20they%20are%20collaborating%20on,less%20than%201%20percent%20successful.

There is a further concern as to the genetic dangers that would be inherently present in the cloning process. Not only does the cloning process have a low success rate, but the viable clone also suffers an increased risk of serious genetic malformation, cancer, or a shortened lifespan. [8] Cloned animals display many genetic deformities that do not often occur in natural births. The human genome is far more complex than many creatures that have presently been birthed by reproductive cloning. The researchers that cloned the famous "Dolly the Sheep" created more than two hundred failed subjects or subjects so genetically deformed that they had to be euthanized. [9] If such results were similar in the cloning of humans, no secular scholar would consider the birth of genetically malformed offspring to be appropriate. Such births would be a source of great harm to the cloned individual and are generally considered unacceptable.

Both the generalized risk of death and the risk of genetic deformity in the cloning process would violate the general principle that no harm be done. How can it be said that the cloned individual has any benefit in the cloning process? There can be no benefit to the cloned individual if death or gross deformity is a result of the process. Until the process itself is safer, the secular view would object to reproductive cloning for these reasons. Each of the additional risks below has the same fate and response as the risk of physical harm.

b) Dangers to Mental Health

Scientists fear cloned individuals would be at high risk for the development of mental health deficiencies. Most concerns lie in the realm of identity issues that the potential cloned organism may face. The fear is that in individuals originating from the transfer of an adult's nucleus, the knowledge that one is the result of cloning may diminish one's sense of uniqueness. [10]

---

[8] Savulescu, Julian, *Should we clone human beings? Cloning as a source of tissue for transplantation*, 25 J. of Med. Ethics. 87, 95 (1999)
[9] Weldon, Dave. *Why Human Cloning Must Be Banned Now*, 8(1) Dignity 1-4 (2002)
[10] Morales, Nestor, *Psychological and Ideological Aspects of Human Cloning: A Transition to a Transhumanist*

This concern is comparable to the feelings that adopted children and children born as the result of artificial incrimination often have a desire to know more about their birth parents. This desire has been repeatedly linked to various mental health concerns including clinical depression in these children. [11] Given the lack of research, many fear that a cloned individual would have significant hurdles with its mental health as it develops. The cloned individual would struggle to conform to the very essence of its existence; the thought of being the first being born by such means would be immeasurable. Such a risk of harm is so great that many scholars turn to this argument in their rejection of reproductive cloning.[12]

Perhaps most significant to the various mental health concerns within the cloning process is the overall risk to a cloned individual's sense of identity. The problem would be magnified if there were multiple cloned individuals of the same genetic mother or father. Such a problem could arise even because of a potential resemblance to a cloned individual's genetic parent.[13] Such a resemblance is certain, and a struggle with identity is almost evident. Such a thought is comparable to the identity struggles that genetically similar or identical twins often suffer from.

Research shows that the development of a positive, independent identity during adolescence is more difficult for twins than for singletons because they have to extricate themselves from their parent's control and co-twin's control.[14] Such struggles tend to lead to mental health concerns for twins. The same issues might arise due to similar influences on a cloned individual's developmental identity. The general understanding within scientific thought

Psychology, 20 J. of Evolution and Tech 19-42 (2009)

[11] Hart R., Norman R.J., *The longer-term health outcomes for children born as a result of IVF treatment. Part II-- Mental health and development outcomes,* 19(3) Hum. Reprod. Update 244-250 (2013)

[12] Brock, D.W, *Human cloning and our sense of self,* 296 Sci. 314-316 (2002).

[13] Willem-Jan van der Wolf, Relinde van Laar, *Cloning and Stem Cell Research: Legislative Developments in Stem Cell Research in the United States of America,* Vol. I.2 P.1, p. 244 (2008)

[14] Malahat Amani & Arefeh Shariatipour, *Comparison of Self-Differentiation and Identity Statuses in Twins and Nontwins,* 24 Twin Research and Human Genetics 176–183 (2021).

is that a cloned individual would be at high risk of identity disorders and other mental health concerns in the same way that identical twins are. The risk of parental narcissism and the "replacement child" effect are also high.[15] Popular thought is, apparently subconsciously, a parent of a cloned individual could view the child as a pure copy of themselves and act as an absolute expert on the child's development; this could lead to the parent not understanding the wants or feelings of the cloned child and, in turn, lead to grave mental health risks.[16]

As such, the secular community decries this risk to the mental health of the cloned individual as a form of unjustifiable harm, and this reason is often used as an objection to the practice of cloning in general.

c) **Danger to the Structure of Family**

It is a foolish prospect to assume that a cloned individual would not receive the necessary love and nurturing care that any normal child would. Many children around the world are taken into families by alternative means like adoption or in vitro fertilization and are given the appropriate care required to raise a child. However, the key difference presented by the cloning process would be the fact that there would exist a one-sided and replicative biological connection to only one parent.[17] As such, it can be assumed that cloning presents a new challenge to the traditional familial structure that is not present in adoption or in vitro fertilization. The argument essentially rests on the assertion that the cloned individual would introduce a dynamic that has not yet been tested in the modern family.

---

[15] Stephen E. Levick, *Psychological Aspects of Human Reproductive Clones: What Can We Infer From the Clone-Like,* 23 Psychiatric Times 14 (2006).
[16] *Id.*
[17] David Orentlicher, *Cloning and the Preservation of Family Integrity*, 59 LA. L Rev. (1998)

Such a risk is generally considered speculative, and some secular writers would disagree with this being considered a risk factor to consider in human cloning.[18] These secular writers argue that reproductive cloning is a useful tool for creating families in the same way in vitro fertilization is used. This is a particularly useful argument when considering both the homosexual relationship and other modern relationships where producing a child naturally is simply not possible. However, both sides of the argument will freely admit that the act of reproductive cloning breaks natural boundaries between generations and that there is a risk that cloning could strain existing social ties in the model of the traditional family.[19]

d) The Minority Position:

While the majority of secular writers have concluded that reproductive cloning is not ethical and should not be allowed under any circumstance, there is a minority that maintains that there are some situations in which the practice may be considered to be ethical. It should be noted here that there are far more secular writers who see therapeutic cloning as an ethical practice; however, the divide is significantly smaller when dealing with the topic of reproductive cloning.

Even scholars who argue that the practice of cloning is ethical raise the issue of physical harm to the cloned individual. The reasoning of the minority is typically that the practice remains unethical until the risk of anomalies and death are resolved in the cloning process.[20] However, the minority suggests that should the efficacy of the practice improve and the rate of harm decline, the majority of the main arguments against the practice will fail.[21]

---

[18] *Id.*

[19] Willem-Jan van der Wolf, Relinde van Laar, *Cloning and Stem Cell Research: Legislative Developments in Stem Cell Research in the United States of America*, Vol. I.2 P.1, p. 256 (2008)

[20] Carson Strong, *The ethics of human reproductive cloning*, 10 Reprod. BioMedicine Online 45-49 (2004)

[21] Kerry Macintosh, Illegal Beings: Human Cloning and the Law 64 (2005)

One such argument used in support of cloning is the plight that infertile couples suffer by not being physically able to have children. The minority thought is that safe cloning would provide an alternative to practices such as in vitro and leave the parents with a child that is genetically related to at least one of its parents.[22] This view would essentially be an extension of procreative freedom arguments that have dominated medical debate in the twentieth and twenty-first centuries. This argument would view the practice as moral for couples that are unable to have children and the argument could be extended in general to other relationship styles where childbearing is impossible, such as the homosexual relationship.

The minority would also attack the arguments concerning identity and dignity as presented above. The argument is essentially that reproductive cloning would not produce two identical people only two people with identical sets of genes; they simply assert that genetic identity neither means nor entails personality identity.[23] This argument has some grounding in reality; even identical twins are capable of maintaining or learning to create their own identities. The minority would consider the identity problem presented here as a fallacy; they suggest that even cloned animals and human twins bear significant differences from each other despite being genetically identical.[24] Examples of this are physical differences such as height, weight, and general appearance.[25] However, as established here, the risk of mental health problems does exist in similar situations, like with identical twins, genetically similar individuals are more likely to suffer from identity issues.[26]

---

[22] *Id.*

[23] Raanan Gillon, *Human reproductive cloning-a look at the arguments against it and a rejection of most of them*, 92 J. Royal Soc. Med. 3-12. (1999)

[24] Macintosh, Kerry, Illegal Beings: Human Cloning and the Law 23 (2005).

[25] *Id.*

[26] Malahat Amani & Arefeh Shariatipour, *Comparison of Self-Differentiation and Identity Statuses in Twins and Nontwins*, 24 Twin Research and Human Genetics 176–183 (2021).

The minority in this field certainly have great points as to moral considerations in the secular field. The arguments against the identity problem and the risk of harm are cogent and often fairly convincing. However, it appears that the minority often misstates the issue that the majority of the scientific community is concerned with. The concerns of the broader community are the risks that are inherent in the process needed to get to a point where the practice is effective and without grave risk; getting to this point will require significant harm to be endured by the cloned individuals. This is the summation of the divide between the majority and minority positions. Therefore, the majority of scientific thought maintains the practice to be unethical despite the objections of this growing minority.

The Religious Objections

Given an analysis of the nature of the secular concerns above, a detailed analysis demands that the religious views on cloning must be considered so that this survey may be complete. This article will therefore continue by briefly analyzing the various religious schools of thought on the matter. For simplicity, only the views of the world's three most dominant religious groups will be addressed here. At present, the three largest religious movements in the world are Christianity, Islam, and Hinduism.[27] As such, the general views of these religious groups will be discussed below.

a) Christianity

Christianity is a religion founded early in the first century and has long remained the world's most prevalent religious faith. As of 2017, there were over two billion Christians worldwide.[28] Christians believe that the Messiah from Jewish religious prophesies, Jesus Christ,

---

[27] Conrad Hackett and David Mcclendon, *Christians remain world's largest religious group, but they are declining in Europe*, Pew Research Center, (Oct. 11, 2023 6:00 PM) https://www.pewresearch.org/short-reads/2017/04/05/christians-remain-worlds-largest-religious-group-but-they-are-declining-in-europe/. (2017)

came to earth early in the first century and was sacrificed as a gift to the world. Christians follow the teachings of Jesus as well as some aspects of the older Jewish religion. Christian theology has dominated Western thought for centuries and, somewhat frequently, the religious leaders of the religion express their opinion on secular matters; their opinions are typically based on their worldview that is rooted in their holy book, The Bible.

Christian thought on human reproductive cloning is predominantly, somewhat predictably so, opposed to the practice. However, certain Christian writers find the practice, if successful, is permissible. Michael Broyde, a Jewish scholar writing on a biblical thought, has written that cloning is essentially a form of assisted reproduction, much like artificial insemination and surrogate motherhood, and should be made available to infertile couples when it becomes technologically feasible.[29] However, this view appears to be an outlier in the Christian school of thought. The general view is quite in line with the secular view of the issue; specifically that the act is akin to playing God and violating human dignity.

The chief concern of Christianity may be the risk of physical harm that such a cloned individual would suffer. As mentioned earlier in this writing the risk of harm to any potential cloned individual appears to be great at present. It would not be hard for one to imagine that the Christian worldview is inherently opposed to such harm befalling a human life. When considering this proposition, it may be helpful to turn to the popular Christian argument against abortion. In a general sense, the practice of abortion is in opposition and conflict with the values reflected in popular branches of Christianity. The main thrust of this point is that abortion is immoral, and a destruction of a human being created in God's image.[30] Christians in general

---

[28] *The Global Religious Landscape*, Pew Research Center (Dec. 15, 2023 10:00 AM) https://www.pewresearch.org/religion/2012/12/18/global-religious-landscape-exec/ (2012)
[29] Broyde, Michael, *Cloning People: A Jewish Law Analysis of the Issue*, 30 Conn. L. Rev. 503 (1998).
[30] *Id.*

regard even the unborn to have special value and that knowingly causing a fetus harm through abortion is akin to even the grave sin of murder. By comparison, the harm caused to the unborn during an abortion is similar to the harm caused to an unsuccessfully cloned individual. If such a life has intrinsic value in any way, the vast occurrences of death and deformity that would result from the human action of cloning would be considered causing grave harm to a being that has dignity in the eyes of God.

However, there is some concern that such an individual could suffer from a lack of dignity as well. Christians take issue with the act and view it as an act of creation that defiles the nature and creation of God. In support of such thought the Christian would argue that man is a unique aspect of creation and made in the image of God. Biblical passages support this and tend to indicate that there is a specific intrinsic value in human life.[31] Further, the Biblical passages indicate that that value is present even before a human is born.[32] With such value comes an intrinsic sense of human dignity that each human possesses from the moment of conception. Contrary to this core view of human life, reproductive cloning would remove God from the process and create a being that may not have the value of life meant to be imposed upon it by God. Christians would undoubtedly have vast disagreements within various denominations about how such a cloned individual should be treated, but it is doubtful that such a being could carry the intrinsic dignity that humanity was intended to possess. Such an action is almost certainly "playing God' from the Christian perspective and would be an affront to the role God plays in creation itself.

It seems somewhat noteworthy that the Christian opposition to cloning is quite similar to the secular argument against the practice. This fact coupled with the present state of the

[31] Genesis 1:26-27, CSV (2017)
[32] Psalms 139:13-16, CSV (2017)

technology is at a generally unsuccessful stage and seems to have led to low visibility to a Christian argument against the practice.[33] The majority of Christian writing on the subject seems to come from Catholic schools of thought that may not represent all branches of Christianity accurately. However, at the time of writing, this writer could identify only one such sect of the faith that adopts a view that is positive toward reproductive cloning in any way, that organization being the Church of England.[34] It is therefore the position of this writing that the Christian worldview inherently conflicts with the practice of reproductive cloning because such an individual would suffer unnecessary harm that would be an insult to human life in general and because the practice would potentially rob the cloned individual of some measure of inherent dignity.

b) Islam

Islam is a monotheistic Abrahamic religion founded on the teachings of the Prophet Muhammad, as revealed in the Quran, the holy book of Islam. While the religion bears many facial similarities to Christianity, it must be made clear here that the groups do not worship the same God. Islam focuses on the absolute oneness of Allah (God). Muslims believe that there is no deity but Allah, and Muhammad, his final prophet, is the messenger who brought the world the word of God. This is in stark contrast to Christianity as they worship Jesus as part of the same being as God. Islam has held strong throughout the centuries and current estimates find that there are over one and a half billion practitioners worldwide.[35]

---

[33] Zachary Smith, *Christian Response to Human Cloning*, Tennessee Research and Creative Exchange (2001)
[34] Weasel, Lisa H., and Eric Jensen, *Language and Values in the Human Cloning Debate: A Web-based Survey of Scientists and Christian Fundamentalist Pastors*, 24 New Genetics and Soc'y 1-14 (2005)

In the religion of Islam, bioethics is not an independent field of study within the Islamic tradition but a branch of Islamic law and ethics. Thus, Muslims consider their primary authority on the matter to be vested in Muslim religious scholars.[36] Following the announcement of the cloning of Dolly the Sheep in 1997, the Muslim scientific community, led by the Islamic Organization of Medical Sciences and the International Islamic Fiqh Academy, convened twice to discuss the matter, the state of Islamic thought on the matter is largely governed by the conclusions of these conferences.[37] Unlike its Abrahamic counterpart, Islam as a whole is not largely concerned with the dangers of "playing god." Muslim belief teaches that Allah, the creator of the universe, has established the system of cause-and-effect in the world; all creation takes place solely through his own divine will.[38] However, criticism of the practice is present in the religious movement and many Islamic religious scholars prohibit the practice. Such arguments typically arise from the very risks that are presented in the secular objections above; that is, that the technology is far too dangerous to women and embryos. However certain religious arguments do exist and are somewhat complex.

The Quran is the holy text of the Islamic faith and as stated above, many Islamic jurists believe that the text informs law in all areas of life. One relevant passage that informs the subject of human cloning states, "Allah has cursed Satan who said, 'I will surely take of Your servants a settled share, and I will lead them astray and give them [false] hopes . . . and I will prompt them to alter Allah's creation.[39] Some Islamic scholars use this verse to explain that cloning is an

---

[35] *The Global Religious Landscape*, Pew Research Center (Dec. 15, 2023 10:00 AM) https://www.pewresearch.org/religion/2012/12/18/global-religious-landscape-exec/ (2012)
[36] Mohammed Ghaly, *Human Cloning Through the Eyes of Muslim Scholars: The New Phenomenon of the Islamic International Religioscientific Institution*, 45 Zygon 7-35 (2010)
[37] *Id.*
[38] Siddiqi M, *Human cloning: an Islamic perspective*, Crescent Life, (Oct. 11 7:00 PM) http://www.crescentlife.com/wellness/human_cloning_islamic_perspective.htm (2004)
[39] Quran, 4:118-119

offense against the creative will of God and that cloning, along with other practices is an attempt to alter the creation of God. This group would argue that one goal of cloning, the act of improving human genetic make-up, would be an action that is disproportionate to man's flawed nature as prescribed by God.[40] It has been noted that this though is not universal within Islamic jurisprudence.[41] Many writers have now concluded that this is the view a growing minority within the religion.[42]

As with many religious groups, there is a generalized concern about the act of "playing God' within the Islamic faith. Within the Quran, Muslims are reminded that creation itself belongs to God and that he governs life, death, and creation.[43] While there is a generalized concern as to cloning in this regard, the majority of Islamic scholars reject this thought.[44] The prevailing view within Islam is that one "plays God" when the individual attempts to create in the same way that God creates man.[45] Given that God has endowed men with the knowledge to create in other ways, many Islamic thinkers and scientists have grown to consider cloning an act of co-creation that is within the providence of man.[46] Despite the majority view, there do exist Islamic jurists that argue the act of cloning is indeed an act of creation; as appears typical, there is dissension in Islamic Theology on the matter.

However, despite this disagreement as to the generalized theology of the practice, legal authorities in both Sunni and Shiite divisions of the religion have officially banned the practice

---

[40] Nasr-Esfahani, M. H., Ahmad-Khanbeigi, K. H., & Hasannia, A., *Qur'anic Views on Human Cloning (I): Doctrinal and Theological Evidences,* 15 Int'l J. of Fertility & Sterility 73–79. (1998)
[41] Fazlollah SMH, *Human cloning from the point of view of Ayatollah Seyed Mohammad Hossein Fazlollah*, Fiqh. (2005).
[42] *Id.*
[43] *See* Quran 7:54 and 2:258
[44] Mohammad Nasr-Esfahani, *Qur'anic Views on Human Cloning (I): Doctrinal and Theological Evidences*, 15 Int'l J. of Fertility & Sterility, (1998)
[45] *Id.*
[46] Tabatabayi MH, *Al-Mizan fi Tafsir al-Qur'an*, Dar alKotob al-Islamiah (1977)

of reproductive cloning; the branches remained split as to therapeutic cloning. Three essential concerns are identified. Firstly, the jurists remained concerned that there may be a break-up in the family system creating the potential for confusion as to the identity of cloned individuals. The Quran generally defines the bounds of marriage and the sanctity of childbearing within the marriage itself.[47] Such a bond is considered holy, and some Islamic scholars have expressed concerns generally about the impact such an action would have on a family unit. The Second and third concerns focus on the likelihood of illness or death of the cloned individual and the potential danger to the surrogate mothers. Such support for this thought is sometimes grounded in the idea that men are commanded to "not let your own hands throw you into destruction;" the general idea is that reproductive cloning is so dangerous to all individuals involved that it is self-destructive and therefore against this command of God.[48]

In general, there is a theological divide within Islam as to whether the practice can be banned on theological grounds. Islam presents an interesting contrast to religious discourse in other countries because the religious order of Islam touches the law in many countries where the religion is present. Despite the apparent dissension in the current conversation surrounding cloning, the consensus among jurists in Islamic law is that the practice is unsafe and is therefore illegal in every Muslim-controlled country.

c) Hinduism

Hinduism is a diverse and ancient religion that has evolved over thousands of years. It lacks a single founder or central religious authority, and its beliefs and practices vary widely. The Hindu religion is much older than both Christianity and Islam; most scholars date its origin to somewhere in the Iron Age, 1300–300 BCE.[49] Also unlike its Abrahamic counterparts,

---

[47] See Quran 4:1 and 13:8
[48] Quran 2:195

Hinduism is notably a polytheistic religion. Hinduism is also notable for its belief in reincarnation and its use of the ancient texts, the Vedas and the Upanishads, in guiding its beliefs and practices. As of 2017, there were over one billion believers in Hinduism worldwide.[50]

Unlike the two Abrahamic Religions discussed above, bioethics is not a field that many leading Hindu figures tend to focus on. Also unlike the other religions presented here, Hinduism does not hold creationism in high regard. The Advaita Vedanta (non-dualism) philosophy of Hinduism does not separate God from man. Instead, Hindus believe that man engineers divine law alongside the chief architect God.[51] In other words, God executes his will through humans, including Hindu scientists. With this thought, man is often considered to be another creator in Hinduism; many Hindus base this belief on the veridic texts. In one such story a man named Rubhus, attempting to please the Gods, weaves together a perfect human from the very fabric of the God's being.[52] May Hindus consider this to be an example of how humans, when enlightened are permitted to create in the way that the Gods created man. Thus, it would appear that the typical objection to "playing god" is not present in Hindu belief.

However, there is some concern with the practice in the Hindu community. One of Hinduism's central tenets is that of reincarnation. Hindu religious thought dictates that the soul is an eternal object and that when the body dies, the soul lives on and passes to another body. There is the further belief that every living creature has such a divine soul and that such souls eventually reach "Moksha" wherein the cycle of death and rebirth ceases.[53] One generalized

---

[49] Alf Hiltebeitel, Hinduism (1987).
[50] *The Global Religious Landscape*, Pew Research Center (Dec. 15, 2023 10:00 AM) https://www.pewresearch.org/religion/2012/12/18/global-religious-landscape-exec/ (2012)
[51] Mayeda, Sengaku, *An Introduction to the Life and Thought of Sankara*, State University of New York City Press (1992)
[52] Rig Veda 33, (Ralph Griffith, trans.) (1896)
[53] Iskcon Dwarka, *What Is Moksha and How Can We Attain It?*, (Dec. 15, 2023 10:00 AM) ISKCON, https://iskcondwarka.org/blogs/moksha/

harm the community has concerns the status of a cloned human's soul. Hindus worry that either the cloned individual would lack a soul and become a passionless creation or fear that a wayward evil soul would claim the physical body. Further, this line of thought leads to interesting considerations about the nature of identity itself. If every living being soul was created sometime in the far past, how can a body made in a tube carry its soul?

A further concern in this matter would be the effect the practice would have on the "dharma" of the individuals who carry a cloned individual. Dharma is context context-dependent and varies in terms of what varna (class) individuals involved in the action belong to, their jati (caste), age, ashrama (stage of life), and gender. The impact of one's actions manifests as one's karma; any manifest harm that a Hindu may cause could result in negative karma that ultimately throws their dharma out of balance. Hindus would have to consider all harm that they may cause to a cloned individual and how that may, in turn, affect their dharma. If such actions are truly harmful, there would be concern that their dharma would be thrown out of balance; this could lead to some form of punishment in this life or in a future life that the practitioner may live.[54] Given that such choices are individualistic, Hindu thought is extremely unclear on the subject. However, it should be noted that a recent study found that as many as forty percent of Hindu respondents believe the practice to be against their religion; perhaps this belief in dharma is the cause for such concern.[55]

[54] Bowker, John, *The Concise Oxford Dictionary of World Religions*, Oxford University Press (Dec. 15, 2023 10:00 AM) https://www.oxfordreference.com/view/10.1093/acref/9780192800947.001.0001/acref-9780192800947-e-1954. (1954)

[55] Mohd Arip Kasmo , Abur Hamdi Usman , Mohamad Mohsin Mohamad Said, Mohamad Taha & Azwira Abdul Aziz, *The Perception of Human Cloning: A Comparative Study between Difference Faiths in Malaysia*, 7 Rev. Eur. Stud. 178 (2015).

It is important to note that Hindu thought on the subject of cloning is not subject to any strict doctrinal limitations. Hinduism is a very individualistic religion and the ethics concerning matters not specifically addressed in holy texts is often left to the singular practitioner.

The State of the Law

Given the various objections to the practice, reproductive human cloning has faced opposition worldwide and in the United States. The international community, at least partially, spoke to the issue in 2005. That year the United Nations passed a resolution that resolved, "Member States are called upon to adopt all measures necessary to protect adequately human life in the application of life sciences . . . Member States are called upon to prohibit all forms of human cloning since they are incompatible with human dignity and the protection of human life."[56] Of note, this vote was not decided on a majority basis as more than thirty member states abstained from voting on the resolution. Further, such resolutions are generally non-binding on member states. At the date of this writing, over 30 countries, including France, Germany, and Russia, have banned human cloning altogether. Fifteen countries, such as Japan, the United Kingdom, and Israel, have banned human reproductive cloning, but permit therapeutic cloning.[57] There are several countries, including the United States, in which no federal regulation or policies exist concerning reproductive human cloning.[58]

Within the United States, there is currently no federal ban on reproductive cloning. However, there have been several notable attempts to regulate the practice at the federal level. In 1998, Bill Frist mentioned earlier, and Judd Greg introduced a bill in the United States Senate

---

[56] G.A. Res. 59/280, ¶¶7, 8, A/RES/59/280. (Mar. 23, 2005)
[57] Kathryn Wheat and Kirstin Matthews, *World Human Cloning Policies*, (Oct. 11, 2023, 4:30 PM), https://www.ruf.rice.edu/~neal/temp/ST%20Policy/index/SCBooklet/World.pdf
[58] *Id.*

proposing a complete ban on human cloning.[59] While being generally supported by the American public, the bill garnered some level of dissent because of the broad scope of the proposed legislation. Senator Kennedy led the opposition claiming that because the bill banned both reproductive and therapeutic cloning, it was overly broad and beyond the scope of what the public supported at that time.[60] That initial bill died where it started in the Senate; while several executive guidelines have been released in the interim, no attempt to regulate the practice at the federal level has been successful at the date of this writing. It should be noted that, at the time of writing, it is against federal policy to fund research on human cloning with federal funds.[61]

However, the practice does seem to be regulated somewhat frequently at the state level. These states can be divided into three distinct groups. The first group, comprised of about half of the states, has not passed any regulation concerning cloning in any form. The second group is comprised of eight states; this group bans human cloning for any purpose. One such state is the Commonwealth of Virginia; the relevant statute provides, "No person shall (i) perform human cloning or (ii) implant or attempt to implant the product of somatic cell nuclear transfer into a uterine environment so as to initiate a pregnancy or (iii) possess the product of human cloning or (iv) ship or receive the product of a somatic cell nuclear transfer in commerce for the purpose of implanting the product of somatic cell nuclear transfer into a uterine environment so as to initiate a pregnancy."[62] This statute is a fair representation of the law in states that have a full ban on the practice. Such states provide varying penalties for violations of the acts. In some states, like Arkansas, violations of the ban are misdemeanors.[63] Other states, like Virginia, such a violation is a civil penalty with each violation costing more than $50,00 in most of these states.[64]

---

[59] *Congressional Record,* February 9, 1998, S513-514
[60] *Id.*
[61] H. Rept. 105-239 - Human Cloning Research Prohibition Act, H.Rept.105-239, 105th Cong. (2023).
[62] Va. Code. Ann. § 32.1-162.22
[63] Ark. Code § 20-16-2204

The third group of states takes a more nuanced approach to the matter and has so-called "clone and kill" laws. Such laws forbid the use of reproductive cloning in childbirth, but permit the practice for research, so long as the organism is destroyed. One such state is California; the relevant statute provides that "cloning is illegal;" however, the statute defines cloning as, "the practice of creating or attempting to create a human being by transferring the nucleus from a human cell from whatever source into a human or nonhuman egg cell from which the nucleus has been removed for the purpose of, or to implant, the resulting product to initiate a pregnancy that could result in the birth of a human being."[65] In a few of these states, such as California, there is no discernable criminal or civil penalty for violating the code.[66]

Currently, no scientific group or individual has been charged with violating any such code. One explanation for this is the presence of a common exception that is found in states even with complete bans. One such statute reads, "This act shall not be construed to restrict biomedical and agricultural research or practices unless expressly prohibited herein, including research or practices that involve the use of (i) somatic cell nuclear transfer or other cloning technologies to clone molecules, including DNA, cells, or tissues; (ii) gene therapy; or (iii) somatic cell nuclear transfer techniques to create animals other than humans"[67] Further, courts have generally attempted to steer clear of the issue. One court, when asked to decide upon the definition of cloning within a given act, declined, and found that the question was purely left to the political sphere.[68] Another explanation for the lack of developments in this area is the consensus worldwide that the practice is unethical. While positive law is present, there has been no true test to many of the governing statutes in question.

---

[64] Va. Code. Ann. § 32.1-162.22
[65] Cal. Health & Safety Code § 24185
[66] *Id.*
[67] Va. Code. Ann. § 32.1-162.22
[68] *Missourians Against Human Cloning v. Carnahan*, 190 S.W.3d 451 (Mo. Ct. App. 2006).

Further, there seems to be some question as to whether cloning bans are even constitutional. Kerry Macintosh, a professor at Santa Clara University School of Law, believes that the state legislation would have a disparate impact on the cloned individuals and that such legislation has a discriminatory purpose.[69] She posits that in its current form, the California statute above may violate the Equal Protection Clause of the Constitution.[70] The argument is essentially that cloned individuals are a class of people, the same as any other existing being, and that limiting the nature of their very existence is unconstitutional.[71] Such Constitutional concerns are perhaps well founded, as no such ban in the United States has been tested. Just as the Supreme Court's decision in *Roe v. Wade* upended settled state law as to abortion so too could be the effect of a future constitutional challenge to existing cloning laws.

This may present a problem in the future; should reproductive cloning become either accepted or the practice expand despite public outcry, these acts will be freshly tested. If the acts are declared invalid or are simply ignored, there will be clear harm felt by the public at large. There is a clear and present need for strong international, federal, and individual state action should the governments wish to combat the dangers of reproductive cloning.

The Possible Solutions

a) Resolution by Law in America

The practice of human reproductive cloning continues to be controversial, and, as described above, the majority of both religious and secular groups find that the practice conflicts with their worldview in some way. This is a somewhat rare instance of agreement between the two groups that has led to a near condemnation of the practice as a whole. Perhaps this

---

[69] Kerry Macintosh, Illegal Beings: Human Cloning and the Law 149-174 (2005).
[70] *Id.*
[71] *Id.*

concurrence is why, at least on the international level, the practice remains largely illegal. However, turning to the United States, the practice has not yet been subject to legislation at the federal level. While the states have certainly attempted to govern this field of law, their statutes remain untested and could potentially be invalidated at any given point in the future.

The need for strong action in this field is evident. The ethical problems surrounding the practice of cloning are vast and are well-known in the scientific community. The ethical issues concerning the mental health and identity of the cloned individual and the great risk of harm inherent in the process seem to be the most common concerns. While state laws do address these issues, this writer will argue that they either do not go far enough or that they are potentially invalid under the Constitution. The absence of federal law on this issue is outstanding when one considers that the vast majority of the international community has addressed the issue and determined that the detriment of the practice does not outweigh the benefits at this time.

The United States should follow this view and propose strong legislation to address the very real moral concerns of this practice as a whole. Congress has had such opportunities before in both 1998 and 2003; they failed to pass legislation at either time. Bill Frist was right; cloning is a problem that forces the government to address the rapid-fire onslaught of new scientific technological innovation that has to be assimilated into our ethical-social fabric.[72] The governments of the world have responded to the concerns of various religious groups (like the ones mentioned in this writing) and to the broader concerns of the scientific community by condemning and outlawing the practice. As the feasibility of this practice continues to increase, it is clear that the United States should follow suit at the federal level.

---

[72] *Congressional Record,* February 9, 1998, S513-514

With this, the solution presented here is that Congress must act on the issue and, at the least, ban reproductive cloning nationwide. Constitutional issues aside, the action would be definite and end the debate within the states themselves as state laws would be preempted by federal action on the issue. Should the government act and take action to ban reproductive cloning, one of the most ethically concerning issues of the modern age will be, at a minimum, foreclosed for a short time. With any luck, the issue will be permanently foreclosed in the United States.

b) Reconciling Religious Thought

The survey of religious attitudes toward the practice of cloning is fairly similar in application; specifically, all three groups discussed here raise objections to the practice and disapprove of the practice in general. Christianity and Islam carry the most similar arguments. While the two groups disagree about the concept of "playing God," the two agree that the process of cloning is inherently harmful and potentially damaging to the dignity of the cloned individual. Leadership in both groups is opposed to the practice and this opposition is found in nearly all sects and denominations within the religions.

In contrast, Hindu belief is far less concerned with the idea of "playing God;" they simply do not believe in such a concept. However, the practitioners of the religion are certainly concerned with the idea of identity and harm to a cloned individual. Hindus fear consequences in this life and future lives for their actions in this field and many have chosen to stand in opposition to the practice for those reasons. However, the very nature of the religion makes ascertaining a generalized belief somewhat difficult; the beliefs of Hindus vary wildly and as such there are groups for and against the practice.

Reconciling the views of these various groups is easier here than it would be on other issues present today. Given that all three present some concern over the harm to the cloned individual, they would appear to hold remarkably similar beliefs on the subject. Except for Hindu and Islamic scholars who object to the idea of "playing god," there is not much material difference in ideas present here. The debate surrounding human reproductive cloning therefore presents a unique area where the majority of these groups have the potential to come together and advocate against the practice. Religious groups, particularly the Christian right have had a great deal of success in lobbying for their moral concerns on such issues; there is no reason to think the same cannot be achieved in this field.

Conclusion

In summary, the debate surrounding human cloning raises many ethical concerns that both the secular community and religious communities object to. The present risk of harm is great, current statistics show that cloning animals has a thirty percent success rate; the unsuccessful individuals often suffer extreme deformation or death. This death or deformation rate, if present in human subjects, is far too great at this time; the secular community would consider this harm to be perhaps the most significant reason for banning the practice Further, the secular community raises valid concerns as to potential identity and mental health issues that could be present in cloned individuals. Again, the risk of harm in this area is far too great.

The religious communities worldwide also consider the practice to be contrary to their worldviews. The Christian community, almost universally, condemns the practice of playing God; the community also takes issue with the risk of harm to the cloned individuals and the harm to the dignity of those individuals. Similarly, the Islamic community seems to be opposed to the practice. Islamic thought takes less issue with the concept of "playing God" and appears to be far more concerned with the potential harm to a cloned individual. They also remain concerned about potential breaches of the fabric of nature itself.

Contrary to this, Hindu belief seems far more relaxed about the matter. Hindus are far more concerned about the potential harm caused to the individual and how it may affect their present or future lives by way of dharma. Therefore, this debate has presented a rare moment where the majority of secular and religious thought seem to be opposed on the same issue.

However, despite this near-unanimous agreement and worldwide action on the issue, the United States has failed to take strong action against the practice of reproductive cloning. The states have attempted to regulate the matter, but these laws are inconsistent at best and unconstitutional at worst. This writer has therefore proposed that Congress act and adopt a bill similar to the initial proposals by Bill Frist and Judd Greg and ban the practice nationwide. Such action should create criminal and civil liability for violations. Such an action would also foreclose one of the most ethically challenging problems humanity faces in the modern age.

Moot Court Brief – Spring 2023

UNITED STATES DISTRICT COURT
FOR THE DISTRICT OF BLUE RIDGE

CAMERON WALKER FIREWORKS, LLC,	)))	
Plaintiff,	))	
v.	))	Civil Action No. 5321-cv-9412
PUFFIN FIREWORKS, INC.,	)))	
Defendant.	))	

MEMORANDUM IN SUPPORT OF MOTION TO DISMISS PLAINTIFF'S CLAIMS

I. Introduction

This court should dismiss the plaintiff's claims for lack of personal jurisdiction or in the alternative because the plaintiff has failed to state a claim upon which relief can be granted within the scope of the Lanham Act. Concerning personal jurisdiction, this jurisdiction allows a court to exercise its power over a nonresident defendant only when doing so would not be inconsistent with due process. Due process requires evidence that the defendant has purposefully availed itself to the forum state, that the defendant has "minimum contacts," and that the exercise of jurisdiction is reasonable. However, Puffin Fireworks has not purposefully availed itself and nor has it established any minimum contacts with the forum state. Therefore, exercising personal jurisdiction would be improper.

Lanham Act claims require that the defendant make a statement of fact and that that statement be false or misleading. Puffin Fireworks has not made a statement of fact because the statements in question are non-actionable puffery. Further, even if the statements are taken by the court to be statements of fact, they are not misleading. The statements are in not the sort of statements that can be held to be misleading, and some are even empirically true. For these and the forgoing reasons, this court should dismiss the plaintiff's claims for lack of personal jurisdiction or, in the alternative, for failure to state a claim under the Lanham Act.

II. Statement of Facts

Puffin Fireworks, Inc. ("Puffin Fireworks"), is a manufacturer of fireworks that is headquartered in Canada and has its principal place of business in Ottawa, Ontario. Puffin Fireworks does not and has never sold fireworks directly to consumers in any country. Aff. Robert Wilson ¶ 10. The company maintains its business by selling its product to distributors in more than 150 countries. Pl. Compl. ¶¶ 23, 26. These distributors sell the fireworks within retail stores around the world. Because of this ongoing relationship with their distributors, Puffin Fireworks has never contacted any retail store or any retail customer in any of these global markets. Aff. Robert Wilson ¶ 13. In addition to providing these distributors with fireworks to sell to retailers, Puffin fireworks provides a sufficient amount of marketing materials to their distributors. Aff. Robert Wilson ¶ 40. The distributors are required by contract to deliver the marketing materials to the various retail markets they sell the product in. Pl. Compl. ¶ 27. These distributors are also required to report on the quality of the fireworks to Puffin Fireworks. Aff. Robert Wilson ¶ 18.

The distributor that sells the fireworks in the United States is American Distributors, Inc. Puffin Fireworks has maintained this relationship for over 30 years and is currently under a distribution agreement with the company until the end of 2027. Aff. Robert Wilson ¶¶ 26, 28. The distributor is located and headquartered in New York; this is where Puffin Fireworks sends its product to be distributed. Pl. Compl. ¶ 24. Because of the nature of this relationship, Puffin Fireworks is wholly unaware of which specific stores sell its product or which states American Distributors chooses to sell the fireworks. Aff. Robert Wilson ¶ 12. In any case, the fireworks and promotional materials were distributed in the state of Blue Ridge. The fireworks are sold alongside plaintiffs in a couple of stores. Pl. Compl. ¶ 33, 34. The stores displayed the fireworks and played the promotional material provided by American Distributors on closed-circuit televisions in their stores. Pl. Compl. ¶ 37.

These promotional materials contained opinions designed to market and sell the product to consumers. One such statement claimed that the fireworks are exceptionally safe because the company is not aware of any injuries that have been caused by the fireworks. Pl. Compl. ¶ 38.

Other opinions include statements as to the loudness of the fireworks and that the product would not disappoint the consumer. Pl. Compl. ¶¶ 41, 44. The company made these statements under the opinion that they were true. Puffin's CEO has stated, "I [would not] allow any material I knew to be false to be included in the promotional materials." Aff. Robert Wilson ¶ 45. Further, the statement claiming that fireworks are louder has been empirically proven to be true. Pl. Compl. ¶¶ 49-50. In response to these statements, the plaintiff has made attempts to quantify customer confusion in Blue Ridge by way of surveys. Pl. Compl. ¶ 53.

On November 10, 1997, Puffin Fireworks was notified by American Distributors that the fireworks had a defect and needed to be recalled. Aff. Robert Wilson ¶ 35. The recall was promptly completed. Because of the defects, the company has improved and corrected the design of the fireworks so that they may again be appropriate for sale in the United States. Aff. Robert Wilson ¶ 37. American Distributors did not notify the company of the death of Ms. Lisa Carter and likewise, the story printed in the Blue Ridge Times had no bearing on the company's decision to recall the fireworks. Aff. Robert Wilson ¶ 36.

III. Motion to Dismiss Standard

The plaintiff has the ultimate burden to demonstrate that the court has personal jurisdiction over the defendant by a preponderance of the evidence. *Mylan Labs., Inc. v. Akzo, N.V.*, 2 F.3d 56, 60 (4th Cir. 1993). The judge considers the jurisdictional challenge to determine whether the plaintiff has demonstrated a prima facie case of personal jurisdiction. *Id.* at 60. The plaintiff must demonstrate that the State is authorized to act under its long-arm statute and that the exercise of jurisdiction over the defendant would comply with the Due Process Clause of the United States Constitution. *Id.* at 60. A federal court may only exercise personal jurisdiction over a defendant in a manner consistent with state law. *Young v. New Haven Advocate*, 315 F.3d 256, 261 (4th Cir. 2002).

A Fed. R. Civ. P. 12(b)(6) motion is analyzed through a test expressed in *Ashcroft v. Iqbal*, 556 U.S. 662 (2009) and *Bell Atlantic Corp. v. Twombly*, 550 U.S. 544 (2007). A claim that provides only labels or conclusions, recitation of the elements, or naked assertions void of factual enhancement will not succeed. Rather, the facts must plausibly support the stated claim for relief. *Iqbal,* 556 U.S. at 679. The court must first evaluate the facts as true. *Twombly*, 550 U.S. 544. Then, based on common sense and judicial experience, the court must dismiss a claim unless it goes beyond supporting the mere possibility of a valid claim and instead states a valid claim for relief that is plausible on its face. *Iqbal,* 556 U.S. at 679.

IV. Argument

A. This court does not have personal jurisdiction over Puffin Fireworks.

When analyzing whether a court possesses personal jurisdiction over a defendant, three primary components need to be considered. First, whether the defendant has established minimum contacts in the forum state. The court cannot exercise personal jurisdiction if doing so would offend traditional notions of fair play and substantial justice or if the defendant's contacts with the forum state are not continuous and systematic. *International Shoe Co. v. Washington,* 326 U.S. 310 (1945). Additionally, the defendant must reasonably foresee being sued in the forum state. Puffin Fireworks does not maintain any systematic contacts with the state of Blue Ridge, and they therefore cannot foresee being sued there; further, doing so would certainly offend traditional notions of fair play and substantial justice that the test demands be avoided. Additionally, personal jurisdiction requires that the defendant purposefully avail themselves to the forum state. In the absence of this specific availment, the plaintiff may use the stream of commerce test to fulfill this requirement. This test requires, at a minimum, that the alien defendant is aware that a final product is being marketed in the forum state. *Asahi Metal Indus. Co. v. Superior Court of Cal.*, 480 U.S. 102 S. Ct. 1026 (1987). This case demands an application of the stream of commerce test. Blue Ridge requires that the plaintiff demonstrate something more than the mere insertion of a product into the stream of commerce to justify purposeful availment. *Asahi*, 480 U.S. at 112. Here, it is clear that Puffin does not have the additional connections required to meet the targeting test stipulated by the court.

1. **Puffin Fireworks has not established the requisite minimum contacts necessary for the court to exercise its personal jurisdiction**

In determining whether exerting personal jurisdiction over a nonresident defendant satisfies due process, the court will apply the minimum contacts test created by *International Shoe*. The court will determine whether bringing the defendant into the court would offend traditional notions of fair play and substantial justice. *International Shoe Co. v. Washington,* 326 U.S. 310 (1945). The court will also evaluate if the activities of the defendant are continuous and systematic. *Id.* Additionally, the mere foreseeability of connections with the state is not enough, the conduct of the defendant must be such that he should reasonably anticipate being haled into court there. *World-Wide Volkswagen Corp. v. Woodson*, 100 S. Ct. 559 (1980).

It is only fair to exercise personal jurisdiction over a foreign corporation when its affiliations with the forum state are so "continuous and systematic" as to render them essentially at home in the forum state. *Goodyear Dunlop Tires Operations, S.A. v. Brown*, 564 U.S. 915. In *Goodyear*, two boys from North Carolina died in a bus accident that occurred in France. Attributing the accident to a tire that failed, their parents alleged negligence in the design, construction, testing, and inspection of the tire, which was manufactured in Turkey. *Id.* at 920. This manufacturer never sold products directly to customers and instead ran sales through several distributors. A small portion of the product was sold into the state of North Carolina through one of these distributors. *Id.* Further, the company had no place of business, employees, or bank accounts in North Carolina. They did not design, manufacture, or advertise their products in North Carolina. Nor did the company solicit business in North Carolina or sell or ship tires to North Carolina customers. *Id.* Despite this, the lower court exercised personal jurisdiction believing that the stream of commerce test allowed them to exert general jurisdiction over the foreign manufacturer. *Id.* at 922.

The court held that the state court did not have sufficient grounds to exercise personal jurisdiction over the company. *Id.* at 930. The court reasoned that the company's connection with the forum state was greatly attenuated because of the separation the distributors made between themselves and the manufacturer. This was significant because these connections to the state fell far short of the continuous and systematic connections that are required. *Id.* Because of these reasons, this court held that it would be unreasonable to exercise general jurisdiction over the defendant. *Id.*

Here, the situation is very similar. Like the manufacturer in the case above, Puffin Fireworks does not design or manufacture its promotional material in the forum state. Instead, the product in *Goodyear* and the fireworks here have arrived in the forum state by way of a third-party distributor. This is significant because both are demonstrative of connections that lack the "continuous and systematic" nature required by the minimum contacts test. The manufacturer in *Goodyear* could never have reasonably expected to be sued in North Carolina because it never knew its product was sold in the forum state. Likewise, Puffin Fireworks cannot reasonably foresee being sued in Blue Ridge because the facts stipulate that they have no specific knowledge of the fireworks entering the state of Blue Ridge. The mere fact that Puffin

Fireworks knows that its product could arrive in the United States should not justify the exercise of personal jurisdiction in any state in which its promotional materials arrive. Doing so would be unreasonable and unfair. Further, establishing a basis for jurisdiction through such attenuated contacts would create a dangerous precedent that would certainly offend traditional notions of fair play and substantial justice as outlined in *Int'l Shoe*.

2. Puffin Fireworks has not purposefully availed itself to the state of Blue Ridge by merely inserting fireworks into the stream of commerce.

The minimum contacts test additionally requires that the defendant in a given cause of action "purposefully avail" himself to conducting business in the forum state. *Hanson v. Denckla*, 357 U.S. 235 (1958). The placement of a product into the stream of commerce, without more, is not enough to establish that the defendant has purposefully availed himself to the forum state. Further, purposeful availment of the forum's market requires, at a minimum, that the alien defendant is aware that a final product is being marketed in the forum state. *Asahi Metal Indus. Co. v. Superior Court of Cal.*, 480 U.S. 102 (1987). Here, it cannot be said that Puffin Fireworks has sufficiently purposefully availed itself to the State of Blue Ridge. The company has not targeted the forum state and further, Courts must exercise "[g]reat care and reserve . . . when extending . . . personal jurisdiction into the international field." *Asahi*, 480 U.S. at 115. For these and the foregoing reasons, Puffin has not purposefully availed itself to the state of Blue Ridge.

The "stream of commerce plus" test in this state requires a showing that the defendant purposefully directed its actions toward the forum state in some way beyond the placement of a product into the stream of commerce. *Asahi*, 480 U.S. at 112. In *Asahi*, a Japanese company was manufacturing tire valve assemblies in Japan and selling them to tire manufacturers, in Taiwan. *Id.* at 106. The Taiwanese company incorporated the assemblies into its finished tires, which it then sold to the United States. *Id.* The Taiwanese company was sued in California for product liability. *Id.* The company then brought the Japanese manufacturer into the suit. The case was eventually appealed to the Supreme Court on grounds that exercising personal jurisdiction over the company would be unfair. *Id.*

The court held that the company had not purposefully availed itself to conducting business in the United States and therefore personal jurisdiction was not appropriate. *Id.* at 113. The court reasoned that, while the plaintiff had established that the defendant knew the parts were entering the country, they had not established that the defendant had purposefully availed itself to the forum state. *Id.* The mere fact that the petitioner knew that some of its parts would be used in products that would be sold in the state did not provide the necessary minimum contacts for the state to exercise personal jurisdiction over the petitioner, since the petitioner did nothing to purposely avail itself of the privilege of conducting activities in the state. *Id.* With this, the court concluded that exercising personal jurisdiction over the defendant would be unjust.

Here, the facts are remarkably similar to the above case. Puffin Fireworks is a global manufacturer of fireworks that has made promotional material to market its product; however, the company does not provide these materials directly to customers. Instead, the company sells the fireworks to a distributor who then inserts them into the stream of commerce in the United States. However, while Puffin does know that its promotional materials are present in the United States, the company has never directed the distributor to insert the product into any particular state. This is comparable to the Japanese company in *Asahi* merely selling the parts for tires to various distributors. Both companies did not conduct activities, run offices, or sell anything directly to a consumer or store within the United States. This is significant because satisfying certain minimum contacts is required to exercise personal jurisdiction. The court must turn to the stream of commerce test. As Justice O'Connor explained, "a defendant's awareness that the stream of commerce may or will sweep the product into the forum State does not convert the mere act of placing the product into the stream into an act purposefully directed toward the forum State." *Id.* at 112. Further, like in *Asahi*, Puffin did not create the distribution system that brought the promotional materials to the United States, and the company had no control over which states the material was sent to. With this, the defendant has not, other than inserting the promotional materials into the stream of commerce, conducted any activities that indicate purposeful availment under the stream of commerce standard.

3.   **Even if Puffin Fireworks has availed itself, it would be unreasonable for this court to exercise personal jurisdiction in light of fairness.**

To help courts in interpreting fairness, the Supreme Court has provided several factors in *World-Wide Volkswagen Corp. v. Woodson*, 444 U.S. 286 (1980) that demonstrate fairness in exercising personal jurisdiction. These factors are (1) the burden on the defendant, (2) the forum state's interest, and (3) the plaintiff's interest. *Id.* at 292. These factors can defeat jurisdiction if they show that it is extremely unfair to bring a defendant into the forum state. *Harlow v. Children's Hosp.*, 432 F.3d 50 (1st Cir. 2005). In *Harlow*, the plaintiff was referred by a Maine doctor to the defendant's hospital in Massachusetts, where she underwent the medical procedure that gave rise to a cause of action; she returned to Maine and the procedure was paid for from Maine. *Id.* at 53. The plaintiff then filed suit in Maine courts for problems arising from the medical procedure. *Id.* The hospital then removed the case to federal court in Maine and then sought dismissal for lack of personal jurisdiction. *Id.* at 54. They argued, in part, that the reasonableness factors as listed in *Volkswagen* showed that it would be unfair to hale them into a Maine court. *Id.* The court granted this motion and the plaintiff then appealed. *Id.*

The court of appeals held that the lower court was correct in granting the motion to dismiss. *Id.* at 69. The court reasoned, in part, that the factors of fairness demonstrated that exercising jurisdiction would be unfair to the defendant. *Id.* at 67. The court reasoned that despite the plaintiff's obvious interest in obtaining relief for her claim, it would still be unfair to hale the defendant into the state. The court reasoned that the defendant could easily have filed suit in Massachusetts, but simply chose what was more convenient for her claim. *Id.* at 68. The court further reasoned that a vast display of the defendant's wealth was not enough to dispel the burden that would be placed on the defendant to appear in a foreign state. *Id.* In sum, the court found that the factors weighed heavily against exercising jurisdiction in Maine. Given that the contacts were so slight, the court affirmed the lower court's decision. *Id.* at 69.

The facts here are similar to those in *Harlow.* Like the hospital's connections in *Harlow*, Puffin Fireworks has very limited contacts in the state of Blue Ridge. The fireworks are not sold directly to customers by the company; they explicitly go through a distributor. With such a weak showing of contacts, it is clear that the burden to Puffin would be exceptional. To defend this case, Puffin would have to travel more than 700 miles, hire American lawyers, and disrupt the flow of its day-to-day operations with the proceedings. This weighs heavily against the other factors. The plaintiff may very well have an interest in obtaining some form of relief; however, this forum is so unfair to Puffin that this factor is outweighed. Like the plaintiff in the above case, the plaintiff here could just as easily bring suit in Canada or New York, the locations at which the fireworks are produced and shipped. Instead, the plaintiff has chosen a forum to which Puffin has very minimal connections. The forum state here clearly has an interest in protecting its citizens from false advertising. However, this still does not outweigh the obvious burden on Puffin to defend this case. Because this burden far outweighs both the plaintiff's interest and the forum state's interest, the court should not exercise personal jurisdiction

For these reasons, the court should dismiss the plaintiff's entire complaint for lack of personal jurisdiction.

B. **The plaintiff has failed to state a claim upon which relief can be granted within the scope of the protections the Lanham Act provides.**

Within the Lanham Act, an action requires a statement of fact. A court can only find that a statement is indeed a statement of fact if that statement admits of being adjudged true or false in a way that permits empirical verification." *Pizza Hut, Inc. v. Papa John's Int'l, Inc.*, 227 F.3d 489 (5th Cir. 2000). Further, statements that contain exaggerated statements of bluster or boast upon which no reasonable consumer would rely or contain vague or highly subjective claims of product superiority are not actionable under the Lanham Act. *XYZ Two Way Radio Serv. v. Uber Techs., Inc.*, 214 F. Supp. 3d 179 (E.D.N.Y. 2016). Even if a party has made a quantifiable statement of fact, the claim cannot proceed unless the statement is false or misleading. A plaintiff can only show falsity in two ways, (1) literal falsity and (2) not literally false but likely to mislead customers. *Design Res., Inc. v. Leather Indus. of Am.*, 789 F.3d 495 (4th Cir. 2015). If a statement is determined to be literally false, courts will assume that it will actually deceive customers. However, if the statement is argued to be misleading and not literally false, the plaintiff must prove that it deceived a "significant portion" of reasonable consumers. *American Italian Pasta Co. v. New World Pasta Co.*, 371 F.3d 387. (8th Cir. 2004).

1. **The plaintiff has failed to allege sufficient facts to demonstrate that Puffin Fireworks has made a statement of fact because the statements in question are mere puffery.**

The statements made within the advertising materials are not statements of fact within the meaning of the Lanham Act and are therefore not actionable. The claims that the fireworks are "louder by a wide margin" and "the safest on the market" were both designed as vague claims of their superiority. Applicable decisions demonstrate that this type of hyperbolic language is nearly impossible to quantify. Such statements are not statements of fact and are textbook examples of puffery. With this, Puffin Fireworks' statements are entirely sales puffery and are not actionable under the Lanham Act.

Bald assertions of superiority or general statements of opinion are not considered a statement of fact; a claim is only actionable if it contains a specific and measurable claim, capable of being proved false or of being reasonably interpreted as a statement of objective fact. *Pizza Hut, Inc. v. Papa John's Int'l, Inc., 227 F.3d 489.* (5th Cir. 2000). In *Papa Johns*, Papa Johns had initiated a marketing campaign in which the company compared ingredients within their pizza against the ingredients of their competitor, Pizza Hutt. Within these ads, the company used Pizza Hutt's former spokesperson to claim that the customers could taste the difference between the ingredients differences between the brands. *Id.* at 492. The company would punctuate these ads with the slogan, "better ingredients, better pizza." *Id.* While the claims of superior ingredients were acknowledged to be true by the opposing party, they disputed that customers could "taste the difference," and initiated a suit against Papa John's under the Lanham Act. *Id.* at 493.

The court held that while the "better ingredients" tagline was not actionable, the statements as to the preference of customers was a statement of fact within the statute. The Court reasoned that the better ingredients line was indicative of exaggerated advertising. *Id.* at 498 The court found this line similar to a company claiming that its product was the "best in America." *Id.* They further reasoned that the word "better" was simply not quantifiable. *Id.* at 499. They opined that "What makes one food ingredient "better" than another comparable ingredient, without further description, is wholly a matter of individual taste or preference not subject to scientific quantification." *Id.* They reasoned that without a quantifiable attribute, the advertisement would amount to mere puffery. *Id.* The ingredient comparisons were viewed in a different light by the court. They reasoned that no method of interpretation could conclude that the ingredient adds were not quantifiable. Essentially, the court did not question if the comparison of ingredients was indeed a statement of fact. *Id.*

Here, like the statements in *Papa John's*, Puffin Fireworks' language is mere puffery. The statements that the product "won't disappoint" and that the product is the "best on the market" are remarkably similar to the "Better Pizza" line in Papa John's. The statements were puffery primarily because the word "better" was simply not quantifiable. In a similar vein, Puffin's statements that the fireworks "won't disappoint" and are the "best" on the market are demonstrative of language that is not quantifiable. A customer cannot be reasonably expected to quantify what the word "best" means. The statement is exactly like the "better pizza" line, both are wholly a matter of individual preference and not subject to scientific quantification. Likewise, the phrase "won't disappoint" is entirely subjective. No one attribute will assure a customer that a firework will not disappoint them; this is, again, wholly a matter of individual preference not subject to scientific quantification. Further, unlike the ads in *Papa John's*, these statements are not modified by any description of customer preference. Therefore, these statements should be considered nonactionable statements because they fall within the accepted definition of puffery.

Puffery is an exaggeration or overstatement expressed in broad, vague, and commendatory language, and [is not] actionable as false advertising because it is understood as an expression of the seller's opinion only, which is to be discounted as such by the buyer. *XYZ Two Way Radio Serv. v. Uber Techs., Inc.*, 214 F. Supp. 3d 179 (E.D.N.Y. 2016). Further, "puffery" comes in at least two possible forms: (1) an exaggerated, blustering, and boasting statement upon which no reasonable buyer would be justified in relying; or (2) a general claim of superiority over comparable products that are so vague that it can be understood as nothing more than a mere expression of opinion. *Id.* at 183. In *Uber Techs*, the rideshare company had made several statements attesting to the safety and rapport of their drivers. One such statement claimed, "From the moment you request a ride to the moment you arrive, the Uber experience has been designed from the ground up with your safety in mind." *Id.* The company also claimed that they set the strictest of safety standards for themselves and that they worked hard to ensure that we are connecting riders with the safest rides on the road. *Id.* at 184. In general, the statements made by the company frequently stated that they were "deeply committed" to customer safety. *Id.* Considering these statements, a suit was brought under the Lanham Act.

The court held that the statements made by Uber were nonactionable puffery and did not constitute statements of fact. *Id.* The court reasoned that these statements were intended to convey the impression that Uber takes the safety of its passengers seriously. However, how the claims were made was indicative of puffery. *Id.* The court reasoned that the tone of such statements was "boastful and self-congratulatory." *Id.* These boastful statements could not be proven true or false. *Id.* In sum, the court reasoned that because the statements were vague and hyperbolic, the statements made by the company could not be considered statements of fact. *Id.* Because of the absence of a measurable factual statement, the claims under the Lanham Act failed. *Id.* at 187

Here, like the statements in *Uber Techs*, Puffin is intending their statements to convince customers to buy the product. However, the statements are the same type of "boastful language" the court in the principal case held to be puffery. Specifically, the language "From the moment you request a ride to the moment you arrive, the Uber experience has been designed from the

62

ground up with your safety in mind," is of particular interest. Puffin's statement that their fireworks are the safest on the market because they know of no accidents related to their fireworks is made in a similar fashion. And using the test from the court, both are indicative of "vague and hyperbolic" language that is considered to not be actionable under the Lanham Act. Likewise, the phrase "louder by a wide margin" is Puffin's stated opinion regarding its fireworks. The court in *Uber Techs* cautioned against interpreting such language as a statement of fact. Therefore, this language is not actionable, and Puffin's statements and opinions should be up to the buyer alone to discount.

Given that this language is similar to the boastful and self-congratulatory tone in both *Papa John's* and *Uber Techs*, Puffin's statements must be understood as puffery. For these foregoing reasons, the court should conclude that the promotional statements made in the DVDs are nonactionable statements because their nature and content are indicative of the definition of puffery as described above.

2. **Even if Puffin Fireworks has made a statement of fact, the plaintiff has failed to allege sufficient facts to demonstrate that the statements were false or misleading.**

Even if the court concludes that Puffin Fireworks has made a statement of fact within the meaning of the Lanham Act, the court must still dismiss the claims because the statements were not false or misleading. Statements that the product was the best or the safest on the market are not literally false and do not have the potential to mislead any particular customer in making their purchasing decision. The court should therefore conclude that the statements were not false and misleading acts as required by the statute.

A literal false statement is bald-faced, egregious, undeniable, and over the top, and an explicit representation of fact that on its face conflicts with reality. *In re C2R Glob. Mfg.*, Bankr.

63

LEXIS 855 (Bankr. E.D. Wis. Mar. 30, 2021). Further, when an advertisement can be reasonably understood as conveying different messages, a literal falsity argument must fail. *Buetow v. A.L.S. Enters.*, 650 F.3d 1178 (8th Cir. 2011). In *Buetow*, the defendant was a garment company that had claimed that their clothing contained a special carbon fiber that could eliminate all odors. *Id.* at 1186. At trial in the case, an expert testified that the garments did indeed eliminate ninety-six percent of all odors. *Id.* The defense did concede that the garments did not eliminate all odors. *Id.* The district court in this case held that the statement as to the elimination of odors was literally false and enjoined the defendant's use of the statements. *Id.*

The 8th Circuit disagreed and held that the statements were not literally false. *Id.* The court re-expressed that literal falsity within the Lanham Act is reserved for ads that are unambiguously false and misleading. *Id.* Further, the court expressed that literal falsity is measured by what it says to any linguistically competent person. *Id.* The court reasoned that a rational person could not as believe that any product can "eliminate" every molecule of human odor. *Id.* Because of this, the court concluded that this type of exaggeration essentially amounted to puffery. *Id.* at 1187. For these reasons, the court concluded that the statements as to the odor-eliminating qualities of the fabric were not literally false. *Id.*

Here, many of the statements made by Puffin are similar to the statements in *Buetow.* The facts show that the statement "louder by a wide margin" is empirically true because the experiments mentioned in the complaint show that the fireworks are indeed louder than the plaintiff's fireworks. Pl. Compl. ¶ 49, 50. This statement being on its face true defeats any claim of literal falsity because the statement does not in any way explicitly conflict with reality; rather, it conforms to reality. Further, the statements concerning safety are not literally false. Like the statement as to the elimination of odor in *Buetow*, it is not reasonable to assume that a customer would be convinced by the exaggerated claims. Any linguistically competent customer should be aware of the risks that come with using fireworks. Thus, a statement claiming that a firework is "safe" should receive similar treatment to the statement that a fabric eliminates all odors. Statements that the fireworks are the "best" or "won't disappoint" are not quantifiable by any empirical metric and are also therefore not literally false. Given that the statements are not literally false, the analysis here must proceed to implied and misleading falsity.

When determining whether a claim is misleading, the court must view the statements in context; this typically involves the analysis of customer surveys. However, courts have held that if a statement is purely factual and unambiguous, then that statement cannot be proven to be misleading through the use of consumer surveys. *Language Line Servs. v. Language Servs. Assocs., LLC*, U.S. Dist. LEXIS 124836 (N.D. Cal. Oct. 13, 2011). In *Language Line*, the defendant had claimed that it offer[ed] "on-site, face-to-face interpreters." *Id.* at 39. The plaintiff's claim rested on this information. However, later in their complaint, they admitted the information to be true. *Id.* However, *Language Servs.* sought to supplement these truthful facts with customer surveys that showed that customers were interpreting the information on the sight differently than the truthful statements. *Id.* With these facts on hand, Language *Line* moved to dismiss the non-actionable claims. *Id.*

The court held the claims were purely factual and could not be supplemented by customer surveys; they dismissed the claims. The court reasoned that the mere fact that the claims were admitted to be true was enough to exclude the presentation of customer surveys. *Id.* at 40 They reasoned that suppressing the advertisement would make consumers as a whole worse off by suppressing truthful statements. *Id.* at 39. Thus, because that statement was alleged to be misleading only in that it was possible that consumers could interpret it to mean something other than what it did, the court concluded that the statement was not actionable under the Lanham Act. *Id.*

Here, the statement "louder by a wide margin" is comparable to the language and statements made in *Language Line Serv.* In both cases, the plaintiff's complaint admits to a specific statement being true. In *Language Line*, this statement was a certain service was provided. Puffins' comment as to the loudness of the fireworks is similar. The plaintiff's complaint specifically details that, "Defendant's fireworks registered a decibel level of 125; During this test, Walker Fireworks' fireworks registered a decibel level of 90." Pl. Compl. ¶¶ 49-50. Given that numerous courts have held, "that if a statement is purely factual and unambiguous, then that statement cannot be proven to be misleading through the use of consumer surveys." *Mead Johnson & Co. v. Abbott Labs.*, 201 F.3d 883, 886 (7th Cir. 2000); there is no reason this court should not reach the same conclusion as to this phrase. A conclusion in the alternative may make consumers worse off and suppress Puffin's truthful statements, and therefore the court should conclude that this statement is not misleading on these grounds.

When allowing a consumer survey to determine whether a claim is misleading to the public would subject a promotional statement to numerous variables and introduce a high level of uncertainty into the marketplace, the surveys cannot establish that the statements were misleading to the public. *American Italian Pasta Co. v. New World Pasta Co.*, 371 F.3d 387. (8th Cir. 2004). In *New World Pasta*, a dispute arose over the phrase "America's Favorite Pasta." The court held that the statement alone was not a statement of fact and was not actionable under the Lanham Act. *Id.* at 392. However, the plaintiffs sought to use consumer surveys to demonstrate that the advertisement, while ambiguous and not a statement of fact, tended to deceive the public. Specifically, a survey of consumers indicated that fifty percent of the public felt the phrase "America's favorite Pasta" indicated that the defendant's product was a national brand. *Id.* at 393.

The court held that using the surveys to establish an actionable claim was not appropriate because doing so would introduce a high level of uncertainty into the marketplace. *Id.* The court reasoned that allowing a consumer survey to determine a claim's benchmark would subject any advertisement or promotional statement to numerous variables, often unpredictable, and would introduce even more uncertainty into the marketplace. *Id.* The court feared that the resulting unpredictability could chill commercial speech, eliminating useful claims from packaging and advertisements. *Id.* at 394. The court further reasoned that the Lanham Act protects the public from misleading and false statements of fact, not misunderstood statements. *Id.* The court, therefore, concluded that the surveys did little to modify the statements and the statement was therefore not misleading. *Id.*

Here, the statements "won't disappoint" and that the fireworks are the "safest" on the market are similar to the language that was used in *New World Pasta*. These statements are the type of statements that if judged by a customer survey, would subject a promotional statement to numerous variables and introduce a high level of uncertainty into the marketplace. In this case, the customer surveys stated a public opinion that fifty percent of the public had a particular perception of the advertisement. Similarly, the plaintiff's complaint cites a survey that states, "80% of respondents stated that they interpreted a certain brand of fireworks being the safest on the market to mean that no one had ever died because of that brand of fireworks." Pl.'s Compl. ¶¶ 57-58. This survey is being used in the same manner as the surveys in *New World Pasta*. Both surveys introduce a high level of uncertainty into the marketplace. Further, this court should not reward Walker Fireworks for merely relying on people on the street to define what a phrase means. As the court in *New World Pasta* states, "the Lanham Act protects the public from misleading and false statements of fact, not misunderstood statements." *Am. Italian Pasta Co.*, 371 F.3d 387.

The statements made by Puffin are of the same nature as the statement in this case and likewise, the court should not allow the surveys to classify these statements as misleading. Doing so would risk the consequence of introducing a large amount of uncertainty into the marketplace and therefore, this court should not allow these surveys to modify this speech into "misleading" statements of fact.

V. CONCLUSION

For the preceding reasons, the court should grant the motion to dismiss the plaintiff's entire complaint for lack of personal jurisdiction and in the alternative dismiss the Lanham Act claims for failure to state a claim upon which relief can be granted.

RED STAR DRAFT MANUSCRIPT (INCOMPLETE)

2023-2024

Introduction:

In the annals of cosmic history, the saga of humanity unfolds as a tapestry woven with threads of ambition and folly, stretching across the millennia like the swirling galaxies themselves. This is a tale of civilizations rising and falling, each chapter etching its mark upon the vast expanse of the stars. Long before the current age, ancient empires strode boldly among the celestial heavens, their reach extending across the cosmic abyss. From the towering spires of their citadels to the humble hamlets nestled in the shadows of distant moons, they forged a legacy of grandeur and conquest, their ambitions became as boundless as the cosmos itself.

Yet, with the passage of time came the inevitable descent into chaos. Empires crumbled, their once-mighty domains reduced to dust and whispers carried on the solar winds. In their wake, new powers arose, each vying for supremacy amidst the shifting tides of fortune.

In the present age, in the wake of interstellar conflict and political upheaval, the galaxy stands on the brink of another tumultuous era. With the rise of the New Galactic Federation, Mars ascends as the capital of a new order, its leader crowned as the first galactic King. Under the guise of peace, the galaxy braces itself for the inevitable storms of civil unrest and power struggles that threaten to plunge it once more into chaos. And amidst it all, the intergalactic fleet patrols the starlit highways, endeavoring to maintain order amidst the encroaching darkness. The King's decrees are law, his word sacrosanct, as fear becomes the currency by which he maintains his grip upon the stars. In the halls of power, whispers of dissent are swiftly silenced, their echoes lost amidst the vastness of space.

For the common men who dwell in the shadow of this oppressive regime, hope is a fleeting dream, a distant beacon obscured by the smog of despair. The dream of traversing the celestial expanse, once a cherished aspiration of explorers and pioneers, has been relegated to the realm of myth and legend, reserved only for the privileged elite who dance upon the strings of power. Amidst this sea of oppression, the interstellar merchants ply their trade, their ships navigating the currents of commerce that flow through the void. Gangs of vicious pirates kill to profit from the success of these same merchants. Some worlds cling to the vestiges of tradition, their soil tilled by the hands of generations, while others lie barren and desolate, their once-bountiful resources plundered to feed the insatiable hunger of the empire.

Yet, amidst the chaos and despair, there are those who refuse to yield to the darkness. Bands of daring raiders roam the cosmic highways, their ships harbingers of chaos and defiance as they strike against the empire's outposts and supply lines. In the shadows, whispers of rebellion stir, their voices growing louder with each passing day as they dare to dream of a future free from tyranny. In the endless expanse of the cosmos, the faintest glimmers of hope flicker like distant stars, their radiance obscured by the shadows of uncertainty.

Chapter 1: This Planet is a Prison.

Peering through the narrow slits of the transport carrier, Jack's gaze traversed the bleak expanse stretching out before him. Slowly, his eyes acclimated to the muted light, revealing the desolation that surrounded them. Once-proud skyscrapers, once symbols of progress and ambition, now stood as shattered husks, their skeletal frames rising defiantly yet forlornly into the air. The jagged outlines of their crumbling structures etched stark silhouettes against the somber canvas of the early morning, each broken window and collapsed floor telling a silent tale of devastation. The streets, once vibrant arteries of human activity, lay buried beneath layers of forgotten rubble and debris, a grim testament to the passage of time and the unyielding cruelty of conflict. The air was thick with noxious fumes, the acrid smell of the surrounding mines seeping through the slits of the carrier, mingling with the scent of decay and abandonment that permeated the landscape.

Amidst the wreckage, tendrils of thick smoke curled skyward, painting the horizon with ominous hues. Yet, despite the grim scene unfolding before him, Jack remained stoic, his demeanor a mask of calm resolve. Having eluded the clutches of imperial control in the past, he harbored a quiet confidence in his ability to navigate this latest trial. To him, this new challenge seemed merely a variation on a familiar theme, a test of wit and will in a world that demanded constant vigilance.

Jack's heart raced as the armored car barreled through the debris-strewn streets of the once-great city. He can feel the jarring impact of each bump and pothole as the vehicle careens forward with reckless abandon. Despite his well-built frame, balance was lacking in the carrier. Jack griped the nearest handhold tightly, trying to steady himself as the carrier lurches around corners and hurtles over obstacles. Despite the danger, he could not look away from the scene outside the window – the desolate word intrigued him. As the transport comes to a halt, Jack couldn't help but feel a sense of dread. He peered out the window and saw that they have arrived at a massive barrier wall that towers at least twenty stories above them. The wall stretched out in both directions as far as he could see and in front of them is a single narrow gate that seems to be the only way through.

The guards are rough as they unload Jack and the others, pushing them into a straight line. Jack took a moment to survey the area. The gate was fortified with heavy metal doors and

70

reinforced concrete walls. The voice box in front of the gate commanded the guard to enter an identification number, and Jack watches as the man's fingers punched in the seven-digit code. The voice box ordered them to optimize their eyes for a retinal scan. A red beam of light illuminated the guard's face, and Jack could see the man's pupils dilate as the machine verified his identity. It was a strange sight, and Jack can't help but feel a sense of unease as he watches the process. The machine then instructs them to proceed to Gate One for processing. Jack couldn't shake the feeling that something ominous awaits them beyond the gate and can't help but wonder what the future holds for him and the others.

His suspicions solidified as he and the other men were ushered through the looming gate, marking the threshold to their uncertain fate. The atmosphere crackled with tension as they entered the realm of "processing," an ominous term that offered no comfort. The procedure commenced with a harshness that mirrored the grim surroundings. A cadre of guards, clad in nondescript grey uniforms, descended upon them like vultures, their movements devoid of empathy or compassion. With mechanical efficiency, they stripped away the remnants of dignity, tearing the clothes from their bodies with callous disregard. Exposed and vulnerable amidst the sea of other naked men, Jack couldn't shake the chill that gnawed at his bones, nor the uncomfortable awareness of his own nakedness. The cold, unforgiving reality of their plight enveloped him, a stark reminder of their powerlessness in the face of authority.

Amidst the chaos, a solitary guard took control, guiding a small drone with practiced precision. A brilliant green beam pierced the air, casting an eerie glow over the captives. Jack's mind raced with conjecture, labeling it as a "health check" in a feeble attempt to rationalize the invasive scrutiny. ~~Yet, beneath the veneer of reassurance, a sense of foreboding lingered, a silent warning of the trials yet to come in this dystopian landscape.~~

The drone's whirring hum echoed in the chamber, its sleek metal body gliding effortlessly through the air. As it scanned, its cold, calculating gaze swept over the gathering, its sensors locking onto the figures at the far end of the group. A sharp flash of yellow light illuminated their faces, casting an eerie glow against their skin, a stark contrast to the expected green hue.

In an instant, tension rippled through the room like a wave. Without hesitation or a moment for questions, the guards sprang into action. With practiced precision, they drew their swords, the steel gleaming ominously in the dim light. Swiftly, decisively, they moved, executing their duty with ruthless efficiency. The heads of the two men were severed from their bodies, the harsh proclamation of "traitors to the king" echoing as a damning verdict.

As crimson blood pooled on the floor, two other guards swiftly dragged the lifeless corpses out of the room, leaving behind a chilling silence in their wake. The specter of betrayal hung heavy in the air, a reminder of the consequences of defiance in a realm ruled by absolute power.

Then, with a mechanical whir, the drone continued its surveillance, gliding ominously over the assembled crowd. All eyes were on Jack as the light flashed green, relief washing over him like a wave. Yet, beneath the facade of safety, a lingering unease remained, a reminder that on this unforgiving world, loyalty was a currency bought with blood.

The guards, their faces etched with stern determination, swiftly escorted the men out of the cramped processing area and into the expansive heart of the building. Each step they took reverberated through the seemingly endless corridors, Jack's feet echoing against the cold, unforgiving floors. As they trudged forward, Jack's keen eye caught sight of three imposing doors lining the passage, marking the journey through the labyrinthine complex. Emerging through the next gate, they entered a vast courtyard, its expanse extended for what looked like a mile. Above, a terrace loomed, its shadow casting a pall over thousands of tiny cells that lined its edges. It was a scene straight out of his darkest imaginings—Jack had never set foot on a prison world, yet somehow, this eerie scene felt hauntingly familiar.

Ascending the stairs that led to the third level of the colossal chamber, Jack couldn't help but marvel at the sheer scale of their new surroundings. The air was heavy with the weight of confinement, each breath a reminder of the harsh reality that awaited them within these towering walls. Despite the gravity of their situation, Jack's survival instincts kicked in, his irrepressible sense of humor flickering to life like a beacon in the gloom. With a mischievous glint in his eye, he began to banter with his fellow prisoners, his laughter cutting through the oppressive atmosphere like a ray of sunlight piercing the clouds.

But before he could fully embrace the levity of the moment, a firm hand grasped his shoulder, wrenching him back to the harsh reality of their captivity. Spinning him around with a forceful tug, the guard thrust him forward, propelling him towards what could only be described as his new home—a grim reminder of the uncertain future that lay ahead.

Jack's gaze ascended, settling upon the cramped confines of the tiny cell that would now serve as his home. Within its narrow walls, two beds were hewn from the rough stone, flanking a solitary toilet nestled against the back like a forgotten relic. Initially, the cell seemed barren, a desolate echo chamber of solitude. Yet, as Jack's eyes adjusted to the dim light, they fell upon the figure crouched in the far corner.

The man bore the unmistakable marks of a life lived on the fringes of society. Scars etched a map of hardship across his weathered cheeks, his unkempt beard a testament to days spent in isolation, flecks of gray interspersed like whispers of forgotten youth. His countenance, locked in a perpetual scowl, exuded an aura of menace that seemed almost innate—a mask of defiance worn with grim resignation.

Jack's facade faltered as his gaze locked with the stranger's, a chill coursing through him like an icy river. In that moment, pretense fell away, leaving him exposed to the raw truth of their shared predicament. He stood a little taller, a shiver of apprehension racing down his spine, unable to tear his gaze from the man who now occupied his newfound reality.

A ripple of mocking laughter echoed through the ranks of fellow prisoners as Jack was unceremoniously thrust into the cell, their amusement a cruel reminder of the fragile facade he had sought to maintain. Yet, amidst the jeers and taunts, Jack remained transfixed, his eyes locked with those of his newfound companion—a silent acknowledgment of the trials that lay ahead, and the unlikely bond forged in the crucible of confinement.

Jack swiftly donned the garments strewn across the bed opposite his newfound companion, the fabric coarse against his skin as he dressed in the dim light of their cell. With purposeful strides, he made his way to the solitary window nestled in the rear of the chamber. Peering through the grimy pane, he was met with the view of toil and despair—a sprawling vista of thousands of men, their forms illuminated by the harsh glare of mining equipment as they labored relentlessly below.

Turning back to the man, Jack sought to breach the silence that hung heavy between them. "What's your name, old man?" he inquired, his voice a tentative thread woven into the fabric of their shared confinement. In response, he received only a guttural grunt, the old man's gaze fixed on some distant horizon beyond Jack's reach.

With a resigned sigh, Jack retreated to his bunk as the call for lights out reverberated through the corridors, casting the cell into darkness. It was then, in the hushed stillness of the night, that he turned to the old man once more, his curiosity outweighing his apprehension.

" Where are we?" Jack's voice carried a note of urgency, a hunger for understanding amidst the oppressive silence. At first, the old man remained silent, his weathered features a mask of stoic resolve. But then, with a slow, deliberate motion, he turned to face Jack, his gaze piercing in its intensity. "Welcome to Black Castle," he intoned, the words heavy with meaning as they hung in the air between them. "And the name is Creed."

A chill raced down Jack's spine as the truth of their surroundings dawned upon him like a specter in the night. Black Castle—a name whispered in hushed tones, synonymous with despair and desolation. With a curse under his breath, Jack realized the grim reality of their plight: they were not just prisoners, but inhabitants of a world that had long since been forsaken—a barren wasteland, where the very planet itself was a prison, and escape little more than a distant dream.

Chapter 2: "Hey Asshat"

Nestled amidst the cosmic tapestry of the universe lay Black Castle, an ancient bastion forged in the crucible of time—a relic of a world that had borne witness to eons of existence long before the empire's dominion took root. It's very soil, saturated with sulfur, imbued the air with a pungent aroma that clung to the senses like a shroud of despair, a constant reminder of the desolation that surrounded them.

The planet's landscape was a study in contrasts, its barren plains stretching out into the horizon like a vast expanse of emptiness. Yet, amidst the desolation, there was a strange beauty to be found—a haunting elegance in the stark simplicity of the terrain, its rugged contours etched with the scars of millennia past.

The prison world stood as a testament to the King's iron grip upon the galaxy, its formidable walls serving as the final bastion of his authority. From his opulent capital, a mere system removed from the desolate plains that now stretched before Jack, the King wielded his power with ruthless efficiency, his reach extending even to the farthest reaches of the cosmos.

Within the confines of Black Castle, the galaxy's most notorious criminals languished in captivity, their crimes a stain upon the fabric of society. Here, amidst the swirling miasma of sulfur and despair, they toiled ceaselessly in the depths of the planet's mines, their labor extracting dytrite—a coveted resource essential to the empire's insatiable appetite for power and control.

The enormity of the task at hand was matched only by the vastness of the crater that scarred the planet's surface, its yawning expanse covering more than a third of the world's blackened terrain. Within its depths lay untold riches and untapped potential, a tantalizing prize that fueled the relentless pursuit of extraction and exploitation.

Jack's mind drifted to the limited knowledge he possessed about the prison—a patchwork quilt of memories stitched together from the teachings of his father during his upbringing on Centaurus. Education was a cornerstone of life in their world, a value instilled with unwavering dedication by Jack's father, a merchant whose aspirations for his son extended beyond the realm of trade. Under his tutelage, Jack delved into the annals of history and honed his skills in combat, laying the foundation for a future that now seemed inconceivable amidst the desolation of Black Castle.

Yet, his education mattered little in the harsh reality of his situation. The comfortable confines of his past had been shattered by the iron hand of imperial justice. Caught in the web of smuggling, a desperate bid to evade the crushing burden of imperial tariffs, both Jack and his father had been ensnared in a trap from which there seemed to be no escape. As he lay in the oppressive darkness of his cell, Jack's thoughts turned to his father, a figure lost to the shadows of uncertainty, his fate unknown amidst the chaos of their circumstances.

The reasons behind his confinement remained a mystery, a puzzle whose pieces refused to fit together in Jack's mind. Smuggling, though a crime worthy of punishment, typically carried a sentence measured in cycles, not the lifetime imprisonment of Black Castle. The disparity between their crime and their punishment gnawed at Jack's conscience, a nagging uncertainty that refused to be silenced.

Outside the confines of their cell, the ceaseless cacophony of mining echoed through the corridors, a constant reminder of the toil that awaited them with each passing day. The discomfort of his bed added to Jack's restlessness, rendering sleep an elusive luxury amidst the harsh reality of their existence. Turning his gaze to Creed, the hulking figure beside him, Jack marveled at the man's ability to find solace in slumber amidst the turmoil of their surroundings. With a heavy sigh, Jack closed his eyes, willing himself to find respite from the relentless march of time and the weight of this harsh reality.

In the depths of slumber, Jack found himself ensnared in the tendrils of a haunting dream—a spectral realm where shadows danced upon the canvas of his subconscious, weaving a tapestry of despair and uncertainty. In this twilight realm, he stood upon the precipice of a memory, its edges blurred by the mists of time and regret. Before him, his father loomed like a specter, his form shrouded in darkness as he moved with an air of purposeful determination. Yet, beneath the surface, an aura of unease lingered—a palpable sense of foreboding that clung to the edges of Jack's consciousness like a whispered secret.

Jack found himself trailing in his father's wake, their footsteps echoing through the empty corridors of a forgotten world. With each step, the air grew heavier, thick with the scent of impending doom. Jack's heart quickened, a sense of urgency coursing through his veins as he struggled to keep pace with the phantom figure before him.

Suddenly, a shadowy figure emerged from the darkness—a towering silhouette cast against the backdrop of Jack's fractured psyche. With a sudden, swift motion, the figure lunged forward, a glint of steel flashing in the dim light. In an instant, Jack's father stumbled, a pained gasp escaping his lips as he crumpled to the ground, a fatal wound staining his garments with crimson. Jack's cry echoed through the corridors of his mind, a desperate plea for answers amidst the chaos of his fractured reality. Yet, as he reached out to grasp the fading figure of his father, the shadows closed in around him, swallowing him whole as the dream dissolved into darkness.

With a sudden lurch, Jack was pulled from the depths of slumber, his heart hammering against his ribcage like a frantic drumbeat. As he struggled to shake off the tendrils of the dream that still clung to his consciousness like cobwebs, a high-pitched buzz filled the air, piercing through the oppressive silence of the cell. Blinking away the remnants of sleep, Jack's gaze fell upon Creed, the hulking figure standing sentinel by the iron door. Without a word, Creed motioned for Jack to join him, his expression unreadable amidst the dim light of their surroundings.

As the heavy door swung open, a tide of prisoners surged forward, their footsteps echoing through the labyrinthine corridors of Black Castle. With a resigned sigh, Jack fell into step alongside Creed, their path merging with the endless procession of captives that wound its way through the bowels of the prison. Each step brought them deeper into the heart of darkness, the weight of their confinement pressing down upon them like a suffocating blanket. Yet, amidst the sea of faces and the clamor of chains, Jack couldn't shake the nagging sense of unease that lingered at the edges of his consciousness – the dream bothered him.

Jack's fleeting curiosity about their morning excursion was swiftly overshadowed by the gnawing hunger that clawed at his stomach—a constant reminder of the harsh realities of life in Black Castle. Though a part of him dared to hope for sustenance, he knew all too well the grim reputation of the desolate planet they now called home.

Despite the weight of their circumstances, Jack's humor bubbled to the surface once more, his words a feeble attempt to inject levity into the oppressive atmosphere that surrounded them. "Don't you just love summer camp?" he quipped to his silent companions, the words dripping with sarcasm as he attempted to break the tension that hung heavy in the air. Yet, his jest fell upon deaf ears, met with stony silence and disapproving glares from those around him. Even Creed, the silent sentinel at his side, seemed to regard him with a mixture of disdain and disapproval, his gaze a silent warning to temper his tongue.

Abashed, Jack kept his head down as they were herded towards a looming door, its imposing presence a harbinger of the unknown that lay beyond. With a resigned sigh, he braced himself for what lay ahead, the familiar sense of apprehension settling like a heavy cloak upon his shoulders. "Great," he thought wryly, "another carrier."

The vehicle hurtled through the barren landscape of Black Castle with an alarming velocity, its speed surpassing even that of the vessel that had ferried Jack from the distant space dock. As the carrier jostled and swayed, Jack stole a moment to observe Creed, the enigmatic figure seated beside him. Despite the tumultuous journey, Creed appeared unruffled, his eyes closed in a semblance of serenity as beads of sweat trickled down his furrowed brow.

The sheer size of the man beside him was incredible. Towering over him by what seemed like a full arm's length, Creed's presence was imposing, dominating the space around him with an almost palpable force. His broad shoulders stretched wide, straining against the fabric of his worn garments, while his arms, thick with muscle, seemed capable of crushing stone with ease. Every movement he made was deliberate and controlled as if even the slightest gesture held the weight of authority.

Jack simply could not shake the feeling of insignificance that washed over him in comparison. Where Jack was lean and wiry, Creed was a veritable colossus, his frame filling the cramped confines of the carrier as if it were made for him alone. His stature was not just a matter of physicality, but an embodiment of power and strength that seemed to radiate from every pore.

With each passing moment, Jack's admiration for Creed's imposing figure grew, his mind racing with memories of encounters with the giants on the moon of Titan within this very system. But even those encounters paled in comparison to the sheer presence of Creed, whose very essence seemed to command respect and deference from all who beheld him.

As the transport vehicle screeched to a sudden halt, the abruptness of the braking sent shockwaves through its occupants, jolting them against the unforgiving walls of the carrier. With a collective groan, Jack and the others staggered to their feet, disoriented and bracing themselves against the unexpected stop. Outside, the guards loomed, their imposing figures silhouetted against the harsh light filtering through the open doorway. With gruff commands, they herded the men out of the cramped confines of the carrier and onto solid ground. Jack's eyes darted around, taking in their surroundings as he adjusted to the disorienting transition.

To their left, a sprawling vista unfolded—a rugged canyon stretching into the distance, its rocky walls weathered by time and elements. Above them, the dying star of the planet cast a feeble glow, its weakened rays struggling to penetrate the thick shroud of black clouds overhead. Strewn about were the remnants of past labor—worn drills and axes, tools of toil and hardship left behind like forgotten relics. As the guards barked orders, the men were lined up with military precision, each one fitted with a collar—a metallic band clasped tight around their necks, gleaming ominously in the dim light. Jack's stomach churned with revulsion as he recognized the devices for what they were—tracking collars, reminiscent of those used to control animals back home.

"Disgusting," he muttered under his breath, a bitter taste of indignation souring his tongue. Yet, even as he bristled at the dehumanizing treatment, he knew there was no room for protest, no avenue for defiance in this unforgiving landscape.

Under the watchful eyes of the guards, they were methodically paired off, each duo handed their designated tools: a sturdy drill for one and a heavy-duty pickaxe for the other. Jack sized up his partner, noting the weathered lines etched deep into the man's face, evidence of a life marked by hardship. His companion's arms bore the telltale signs of age, muscles once robust now weakened by time and toil. Jack couldn't suppress a flicker of concern; this man seemed ill-suited for the back-breaking labor that lay ahead.

As they began their assigned tasks, Jack couldn't shake the feeling of dread that settled over him like a suffocating blanket. The oppressive weight of their surroundings seemed to sap the very strength from his limbs, leaving him sluggish and drained. Glancing around, he observed his fellow captives, their faces etched with exhaustion mere moments into their labor. Yet, amidst the sea of weariness, one figure stood out—Creed.

With each swing of his pickaxe, Creed seemed to embody the raw power of the Titans themselves. His movements were fluid, effortless, each blow striking true with unerring precision. Jack couldn't help but marvel at the sheer strength and determination radiating from the man, a testament to years spent laboring under the relentless gravity of his home moon.

Memories of his studies flickered to life in Jack's mind, lessons on the physiology of those born and raised in the harsh environs of Titan. He recalled tales of their legendary strength, forged in the crucible of a world where every movement carried the weight of the heavens themselves. It was said that the gravitational pull of Titan imbued its inhabitants with a power unmatched by any other, a strength born of necessity in a land where survival was a constant battle against the elements.

As Creed effortlessly shattered boulders with a single blow, Jack couldn't help but feel a pang of inadequacy. Compared to the Titanian giant at his side, he felt small, insignificant—a mere mortal adrift in a sea of gods. Jack resolved to keep pace - squared his shoulders and returned to his task.

Jack lasted about an hour at that pace. He found himself struggling to keep up with the relentless pace set by the giant. The grueling work took its toll on him, leaving him gasping for breath and muscles aching with every movement. He glanced around, noticing that he wasn't the only one faltering under the weight of their labor. The faces of his fellow prisoners bore the same grim expression of exhaustion and despair, their spirits slowly eroded by the ceaseless toil.

As the hours dragged on, time seemed to lose all meaning, blurring together into a disorienting haze of fatigue and pain. Jack's limbs screamed for mercy, his body pushed to its limits by the relentless demands of their captors. Beside him, several of the older men succumbed to exhaustion, their bodies collapsing under the strain of their labor. Yet, there was no respite to be found, no reprieve from the unending torment of their circumstances. The guards prowled the perimeter with a watchful eye, their electrowhips crackling with latent menace. At the slightest sign of hesitation or defiance, they struck with merciless precision, the crack of their whips echoing through the air like thunder. Jack winced at the memory of the searing pain that lanced through him with each punishing blow, a harsh reminder of the consequences of disobedience.

Despite the agony that threatened to consume him, Jack pressed on, driven by a stubborn determination to survive. He gritted his teeth against the pain, his hands moving with mechanical precision as he forced himself to continue. In those moments of unbearable suffering, he found a newfound strength within himself, forcing himself to make progress in his task.

After what felt like an eternity, the relentless grind of labor finally came to a halt. Jack and the other men were herded back into the carrier, their weary bodies slumping against the unforgiving metal walls as the vehicle lurched into motion. The journey back to the colossal structure from which they had emerged was a blur of exhaustion and pain, each jolt of the carrier a painful reminder of the trials they had endured.

As they were once again marched through the labyrinthine corridors of the facility, Jack's eyes fell upon a door he had not yet traversed. Above it, a simple yet promising sign caught his attention, the words "Protein Dispensary" emblazoned in faded letters. Despite the grimness of their surroundings, a flicker of hope stirred within Jack at the prospect of sustenance, however meager it may be. The door swung open with a creak of protest, revealing a small chamber lined with rows of metal containers. Jack's stomach growled in anticipation as he approached the nearest dispenser, his fingers trembling with hunger as he activated the device. With a soft whir, a small green square emerged – pure protein.

Comment [MOU]: Maybe add some internal dialogue for Jack throughout this area. It seems a little choppy.

Though far from satisfying, the meager ration offered a welcome reprieve from the gnawing hunger that had plagued them for hours. As Jack reached for the meager portion of nutrients, a sudden movement caught him off guard. Before he could react, the meal was snatched from his grasp, vanishing into the hands of a large and more seasoned captive.

" Hey, asshat!" Jack's voice cut through the stagnant air of the chamber like a blade, his frustration igniting into a searing flame of anger. The thief merely chuckled, insolence dancing in his eyes as he sauntered away, his stolen prize clutched tightly in his grasp. But Jack wasn't about to let him get away with it. As the guards began to take notice of the escalating tension, their looming presence casting a shadow over the scene, Jack's resolve hardened. "I said Hey, asshat!" he roared, his voice a thunderous challenge that echoed off the walls. With a swift shove from behind, Jack propelled the thief forward, the force of his frustration driving him to action.

The thief whirled around, fury etched into every line of his face as he squared off, ready to engage in combat. Jack wasted no time, his muscles coiled like springs as he launched himself forward, fists swinging with deadly intent. The first blow struck true, a solid hit to the thief's chin, but to Jack's dismay, it seemed to barely faze him. In retaliation, the thief unleashed a flurry of strikes, each one landing with bone-jarring force. Jack staggered under the onslaught, his vision swimming as he struggled to maintain his footing. But he refused to back down, his determination burning bright despite the odds stacked against him.

Just as Jack prepared to retaliate, to unleash his own torrent of blows, the crackle of electrowhips filled the air. With a searing jolt of pain, Jack was brought to his knees, his muscles spasming uncontrollably as the electric currents coursed through his body. He gritted his teeth

81

against the agony, each blow from the whip driving him closer to the brink of unconsciousness. Another blow sliced against his face and everything went black.

Chapter 3: Creed

Creed's gaze lingered on the scene unfolding before him, his expression unreadable as the guards dragged the limp form of the kid away. It was a familiar sight, one that played out with predictable regularity in the harsh confines of this world. The kid would likely return in a few days, bruised and battered but ultimately resilient—such was the nature of life on this unforgiving rock. For the past few days, Creed had observed the youngster closely, his weathered eyes dissecting every move, every gesture. Like many of the men here, Creed's initial assessment of the kid had been dismissive; another cocky inmate, full of bravado but lacking the hard-earned wisdom needed for survival. Yet, beneath the facade of youthful arrogance, Creed detected a flicker of something else—an underlying strength coupled with some form of raw intelligence.

It was a strength that would inevitably be tested and tempered by the harsh realities of their existence. On this desolate world, where hope was a fleeting illusion and despair an ever-present companion, every ounce of resolve was battered and molded by the relentless passage of time. As Creed reflected on his own tenure on this forsaken rock, a sense of resignation settled over him like a heavy shroud. Ten cycles—a decade of unyielding hardship and unspoken sacrifices. Yet, despite the countless trials he had endured, Creed remained steadfast, his spirit unbroken amidst the ceaseless turmoil of their existence.

As the echoes of the guards' footsteps faded into the distance, Creed turned his attention back to the monotony of his daily routine, his thoughts drifting to the uncertain future that lay ahead. In a world where time seemed to stand still, where the boundaries between hope and despair blurred into insignificance.

Creed trudged wearily back to the cramped confines of his cell, a space that had become his solitary refuge in the unforgiving expanse of this prison world. The door creaked shut behind him, sealing him off from the cacophony of life outside. In the dim glow of the solitary bulb, he settled onto his bunk, the worn mattress offering little comfort against the relentless ache in his bones. Lights out came swiftly, a routine imposition on the fragile semblance of normalcy that persisted in this desolate realm. Yet, even in the oppressive darkness, the restlessness of their existence lingered like a specter, a silent reminder of the ceaseless toil that defined their days.

For Creed, the rhythm of life in the mines was as relentless as the passage of time itself. The mines operated around the clock, their insatiable hunger for labor never abating. And as one shift ended, another began, a perpetual cycle of exhaustion and renewal that echoed through the corridors of their prison. Despite the relentless grind of their existence, Creed considered himself fortunate to be assigned to the daylight hours. In the harsh glare of the planet's dying sun, he found a fleeting respite from the suffocating gloom that enveloped their world. The star hung low in the sky, its radiant rays piercing through the thin veil of the atmosphere, casting long shadows across the barren landscape.

But with the sun's brilliance came danger, particularly for those with fairer skin. The intense waves of solar radiation had a merciless bite, searing exposed flesh with a blistering heat that left behind painful reminders of their vulnerability. Infections from these burns were all too common, their festering wounds a grim testament to the harsh realities of life on this forsaken rock. Men in this world could perish from the very sun that gave it life.

As Creed settled into an uneasy sleep, the distant hum of machinery serving as a discordant lullaby, he couldn't shake the gnawing sense of unease that lingered in the depths of his consciousness.

In the depths of slumber, Creed found himself ensnared in the tangled web of memory and illusion, his mind adrift in a realm of fragmented recollections and haunting visions. As consciousness ebbed away, he was plunged into the depths of a dream, one that seemed to blur the lines between past and present, reality and fantasy.

In this ethereal realm, Creed found himself standing amidst a landscape bathed in the crimson glow of a distant star, its fiery radiance casting long, ominous shadows across the barren terrain. The air hung heavy with a palpable sense of foreboding, as if the very fabric of the universe itself were poised on the brink of collapse.

Before him stood a humble dwelling, its weathered walls bearing the scars of time and neglect. It was a place he knew well, a sanctuary nestled in the heart of a world consumed by chaos and strife. But as he approached, a sense of dread washed over him like a tide, for he knew that within those walls lay the ghosts of his past, waiting to confront him once more. With a heavy heart, Creed pushed open the door, the hinges creaking in protest as he stepped into the dimly lit interior. The air was thick with the scent of smoke and ash, a haunting reminder of the destruction that had torn through his life like an unbridled fire.

And there, in the flickering light of a dying fire, he saw them: his wife, her face etched with sorrow and resignation, and his son, his innocent eyes filled with fear and confusion. They stood before him, frozen in time, as if trapped in a never-ending cycle of despair.

But before Creed could reach out to them, a shadow fell across the threshold, a figure cloaked in darkness and malice. His features were obscured, his presence an ominous specter that seemed to seep into the very fabric of reality itself. With a cruel smile, the figure raised a hand, and Creed watched in horror as a blade materialized out of thin air, its gleaming edge poised to strike. And then, in a heartbeat, the deed was done—the lifeblood of his loved ones staining the floor in a crimson pool, their silent screams echoing in the depths of his soul.

As the echoes of the past reverberated through his mind, Creed awoke with a start, his heart pounding in his chest, his body drenched in a cold sweat. But even as he struggled to make sense of the haunting vision that had gripped him in its thrall, one thing remained clear: the specter of his past would not be so easily laid to rest. And as he gazed out into the starlit expanse of the prison world, he knew that the answers he sought lay shrouded in the darkness of his mind.

As Creed's thoughts meandered through the labyrinth of his memories, they inevitably found their way to the haunting specter of his wife, her gentle smile etched into the recesses of his mind like a fading echo of lost happiness. The weight of his past hung heavy upon him, a burden he carried with stoic resignation, each cycle serving as a grim reminder of the life he had left behind.

His thoughts drifted further, weaving through the tangled threads of his existence, touching upon the gang that had once been his family—the bonds of loyalty and betrayal that had shaped his destiny. For Creed, revenge had always been a guiding force, a solitary beacon in the darkness that had consumed his world. But here, on this desolate rock, surrounded by walls of unforgiving stone and guarded by the watchful eyes of his captors, the notion of escape seemed nothing more than a fleeting illusion—a distant dream that danced just beyond his reach.

With a heavy sigh, Creed reluctantly let go of the fleeting fantasy, allowing it to dissipate like smoke in the wind. The reality of his situation pressed down upon him like a weight, crushing his hopes and aspirations beneath its merciless heel. In this place of endless torment and despair, the very notion of freedom had become a cruel joke—a bitter reminder of the futility of resistance in the face of overwhelming adversity.

And so, with a resigned acceptance born of bitter experience, Creed pushed aside his desires for vengeance and liberation, steeling himself for the endless cycle of suffering that lay ahead. For in the heart of this prison world, where time seemed to stretch on into eternity, there was only one truth that mattered: survival, no matter the cost.

And thus, the ceaseless march of time unfolded, each moment bleeding into the next with monotonous regularity. The labor was arduous, yes, but to Creed, it was a mere shadow of the challenges he had faced on Titan, where gravity held sway with an iron grip. Here, on this desolate world, the weight of the rocks seemed almost insignificant, a triviality in the grand tapestry of his existence.

As he toiled amidst the harsh landscape, the cacophony of labor mingled with the occasional cries of pain from his fellow prisoners, a constant reminder of the brutality of their reality. Yet, amidst the turmoil, Creed's gaze drifted skyward, drawn to the somber expanse of the gray heavens stretched out above him. In the distance, the bustling spaceport beckoned like a siren's call, its promise of freedom tantalizingly close yet impossibly out of reach.

He knew all too well the fate that awaited any who dared to defy the iron rule of their captors. The guards, armed with their lethal slugthrowers, stood as silent sentinels, ready to snuff out any flicker of hope with ruthless efficiency. And so, with a heavy heart and a resigned sigh, Creed turned back to his work, the dream of escape lingering like a wistful memory in the recesses of his mind, a distant echo of a life that once was, and perhaps, one day, could be again.

Time blurred into an indistinct haze, days melding into weeks in the relentless rhythm of prison life. The return of the kid, whether after a mere day or a protracted week, was a flicker of disruption in Creed's otherwise monotonous existence. As the kid reappeared, his demeanor bore the weight of his ordeal, a subtle shift in his countenance betraying the trials he had endured.

Yet, despite the passage of time and the crucible of hardship, the kid's attitude towards Creed remained unchanged. There was still a palpable disdain in his gaze, a silent testament to the lingering animosity between them. Their interactions, always sparse and laced with tension, offered little solace in the desolate landscape of their confinement.

Creed observed the kid's restless demeanor, a telltale sign of the turmoil that plagued his restless sleep. The dreams, no doubt, haunted him relentlessly, their spectral grip refusing to loosen even in the fleeting respite of slumber. As Creed watched from the shadows of their shared cell, he couldn't help but wonder about the demons that tormented the kid's subconscious, a silent observer to the silent struggle that raged within.

The true toll of this prison transcended the physical hardships endured; it gnawed at the very fabric of the mind, leaving its captives ensnared in the labyrinth of their own memories. For the newcomers, this realization had yet to dawn, their innocence a fragile shield against the stark reality of their plight. Here, within the suffocating confines of their shared captivity, memories took on a life of their own, vibrant and vivid as they danced across the canvas of consciousness. Each misdeed, every regret, laid bare in stark detail, a haunting reminder of the ghosts that lurked in the recesses of the mind.

The air hung heavy with the weight of unspoken sorrows, the silence broken only by the occasional shudder of a restless sleeper or the distant hum of the facility's machinery. Shadows cast by flickering lights played upon the worn walls, their shifting forms mirroring the ever-changing landscape of the prisoners' thoughts.

Restless nights became the norm, as the echoes of past transgressions reverberated through the dimly lit corridors. Sleep, when it came, offered little respite, for dreams were but another battleground where the mind waged war against itself. Visions of lost loves, shattered dreams, and irreparable mistakes haunted the slumbering souls, twisting the fabric of reality into a nightmarish tapestry of anguish and despair.

As the relentless procession of days marched on, Creed maintained a vigilant eye on the young newcomer, recognizing the fragile balance between sanity and madness within the prison's confines. Insanity was an all-too-familiar specter haunting these grim walls, its tendrils weaving through the minds of the unprepared like a creeping fog.

In the midst of this bleak landscape, one thing became abundantly clear: the kid possessed a keen intellect that set him apart from the rest. His eyes, sharp as flint, missed nothing, capturing every detail with a precision that belied his youth. There was a calculating gleam in his gaze, a hunger for knowledge and understanding that burned bright amidst the pervasive darkness.

It was not long before the kid's resourcefulness revealed itself in subtle yet significant ways. One day, he unraveled the mystery of the protein dispensary, coaxing it into yielding a double portion with a deft flick of his wrist—a feat that had eluded even the most seasoned of inmates. His ability to navigate the treacherous waters of the mining operation spoke volumes of his cunning; he moved with purpose, carefully plotting his pace to evade the wrath of the guards, his movements fluid and deliberate.

But perhaps most impressive of all was the kid's uncanny knack for survival. In the face of adversity, he remained unyielding, his resolve unwavering even as others faltered under the weight of their torment. When the electrowhips cracked and the older men crumbled, he stood firm, a testament to his resilience in the face of cruelty.

One night a particular dream shocked Creed, images from his past flickered like distant stars in the night sky. Amidst the hazy memories, a figure emerged, shrouded in shadows yet somehow familiar. It was the kid, his presence inexplicably woven into Creed's subconscious. In the dream, they were not on this desolate prison world but in a place bathed in the crimson glow of a red star. Creed's wife and son stood beside him, their laughter echoing in the ether as they walked hand in hand. But the serenity was shattered by the sudden appearance of another figure, a menacing silhouette looming in the distance.

With a start, Creed jolted awake, his body drenched in sweat, the echoes of his dream still reverberating in his mind. Jack's presence lingered, a haunting specter in the depths of his subconscious, a reminder of the intertwined destinies that bound them together in this unforgiving abyss.

As the days stretched into weeks Creed allowed a subtle shift to occur in the dynamic between him and the kid, their interactions becoming a silent language of shared understanding amidst the chaos of their surroundings. Creed found himself drawn to the kid's unwavering determination and resourcefulness, admiring the way he navigated the treacherous waters of prison life with a quiet resilience. There was a fire in the kid's eyes that spoke of untapped potential, a spark that ignited something within Creed—a begrudging respect, perhaps, or even a flicker of admiration.

And as they talked, their stories intertwined like the intricate threads of a tapestry, weaving together pasts both dark and tumultuous. Creed spoke of his days as a soldier, of battles fought and comrades lost, while the kid revealed fragments of a life marred by tragedy and loss.

In the depths of his thoughts, Creed weighed the possibilities, envisioning a plan taking shape with the kid at its center—a daring scheme that could lead them away from this desolate prison world and into the realm of freedom once more. The idea flickered in Creed's mind like a distant star, its light offering a glimmer of hope amidst the oppressive darkness of their confinement. With each passing moment, the allure of escape grew stronger, fueled by the tantalizing prospect of reclaiming what had been stolen from him. His wife, his son, and his revenge.

Creed mulled over the idea of placing his trust in the kid, weighing the risks and rewards of using him as a means to his end. After careful consideration, he concluded that leveraging the kid's skills for their escape was the most pragmatic course of action for the moment. A quick and simple exit strategy, leaving the kid behind once they were off-world, seemed like the most expedient option. The mention of the kid's father provided a potential leverage point, a motivating factor that could ensure his cooperation.

In the shroud of darkness, Creed disclosed his plan to the kid in hushed tones, their voices barely above a whisper. They would orchestrate a brawl in the mines, using the ensuing chaos as a diversion to commandeer a carrier and procure a weapon. With the guards preoccupied, they could make their way to the spaceport unnoticed. If executed swiftly and stealthily, their actions might evade the attention of the authorities. Once at the spaceport, their next objective would be to pilot a ship through the vast expanse of stars, embarking on a journey to locate the kid's father.

It was a risky endeavor fraught with uncertainty, but Creed's determination burned furious like a fire; this was his revenge.

The kid remained unengaged as Creed unfolded the plan, his brow furrowed in uncertainty, his gaze flickering with a mix of confusion and apprehension. When Creed finished, the kid looked at him with a puzzled expression, his eyes locking onto Creed's with a hint of disbelief. "What?" he uttered, the word laden with a mixture of incredulity and disbelief, as if struggling to comprehend the audacity of Creed's proposal. For the first time, Creed grinned.